Southwest Seasons Cookbook

Casa Angelica Auxiliary
Albuquerque, New Mexico

Art by Betty Sabo

To order copies of *SOUTHWEST SEASONS COOKBOOK*,
send $14.95, plus $3.00 for postage and handling, to:

SOUTHWEST SEASONS COOKBOOK
℅ Casa Angelica
5629 Isleta Blvd. S. W.
Albuquerque, New Mexico 87105

For your convenience, order forms are included in the back of
this book.

Printed by Jumbo Jack's Cookbook Co.
Audubon, Iowa 50025

Table of Contents

Casa Angelica

Casa Angelica is a home for severely mentally and physically handicapped children. It provides a loving home and medical care twenty-four hours a day, seven days a week for these special youngsters. Casa Angelica is responsible for the spiritual, physical, medical, emotional, personal, cultural, physio-social and rehabilitive well-being of each resident. In addition to providing quality medical care, programs are developed to enhance the quality of life and individual personal growth of each child.

Casa Angelica was established in 1966, and welcomes children of any race or creed from all over the United States. The fifteen acre home is located in Albuquerque's southwest valley. Casa Angelica is fully accredited, licensed by the New Mexico Health and Environment Department, Public Health Division, with a licensed nurse on duty 24 hours a day, an attending physician available, a staff of nurses, aides, volunteers and the latest specialized equipment.

Casa Angelica is not government funded, but relies solely on contributions. It meets all the requirements established by tax code 501 (C)3. Contributions are tax deductible to the full extent of currently prevailing tax regulations.

All proceeds from the sales of *SOUTHWEST SEASONS COOKBOOK* go to Casa Angelica to perpetuate the loving labors for severely mentally and physically handicapped children.

Acknowledgements

We are most grateful to all Casa Angelica Auxiliary Members and friends who shared their ideas and recipes, and gave unselfishly of their time. A special thank you to our families who have been so patient and supportive.

The beautiful art for this book was donated by Betty Sabo. Her generous donations of oil paintings to Casa Angelica Auxiliary for our annual raffle have realized thousands of dollars of help for Casa Angelica.

In order to offer the widest variety of recipes, ensure consistency of form, and due to the lack of space, we regret that all recipes submitted could not be used.

Dedication

Casa Angelica Auxiliary wishes to dedicate this book to the Canossian Daughters of Charity, lay staff and volunteers who work so diligently at Casa Angelica to care for these special children.

6

Betty Sabo

The award winning oil paintings by Betty Sabo are completed in her Albuquerque Studio from detailed sketches and notes made on location in New Mexico, Arizona and Colorado. A native of Kansas, Ms. Sabo moved to Albuquerque as a child and majored in art at the University of New Mexico.

The Sabo signature is familiar to art enthusiasts throughout the Southwest. She has been invited to exhibit in such varied shows as Margaret Jamison Presents in Santa Fe, The Gallery Show at the Lubbock Art Festival, The Texas Cowboy Reunion in Stamford, Texas and the Mountain Oyster Club in Tucson, Arizona. Her work has been included in the prestigious Rio Grande Exhibit in Albuquerque and in "Magnifico"-Albuquerque Invites. Sabo paintings are included in many corporate collections.

Listed in *Who's Who in American Art*, she has been featured in national publications such as *New Mexico Magazine, Southwest Art* and *Southwest Profile*. Sabo's work is also becoming known to the New York art scene. Her paintings have been exhibited in the National Academy of Design, the National Arts Club and the American Academy in competitive exhibitions sponsored by Allied Artists of America and the American Artists Professional League.

Highly respected in the Southwest, a Sabo painting was presented to President Ronald Reagan by the New Mexico Amigos.

Artist Betty Sabo has added another dimension to her creative talent. She has introduced a new series of collagraphs. A Sabo collagraph was shown in *Print Making in New Mexico*, a traveling exhibit compiled by the New Mexico Governor's Gallery in the Santa Fe Capital building.

Her series, *Children in the Garden*, has been cast in bronze by Shidoni Foundry in Santa Fe and is exhibited in the foundry's gallery. Her paintings may be seen in desk calendars published by *Southwest Art Magazine*, as well as in *New Mexico Magazine's Artists Calendar*, or by calling (505) 255-7375 for an appointment.

COVER PAINTING: WINTERSET

Evening comes to Arroyo Seco, located just north of Taos, New Mexico on the road to the Taos Ski Valley. It is beautifully situated, adjacent to a fascinating, historical area known to explorers from the time of Coronado's journey from Mexico. The area was settled in the mid-1600's. A delightful subject for artists, the clustered adobes around the lovely mission church is typical of the many isolated villages in the mountains of northern New Mexico.

Cookbook Committee

Kathleen Abbott
Shanaz Arman
Janie Armijo
Mandy Arrington
Marilyn Batts
Kathleen Bickel
Darlene Bower
Julia Brown
Geraldine Burke
Rita Carpenter
Norma Curley
Adele Davis
Mary Fanning
Mary Fernandez
Helene Fike
Dorothy Fitz-Gerald
Linda Franchini
Shari Friedman
Louise Gauthier
Selma Gevirtzman
Brendan B. Godfrey, Sr.
Kathryn B. Godfrey
Barbara Henricksen
Lindsey M. Hovden

Nancy Ingram
Christie Kawal
Kate Keith
Gretchen Keleher
Jeri Laxson
Virginia Long
Eugenia Mackie
Mary Ann Munos
Lori Peterkin
Kathleen Raskob
Mary Ellen Rock
Betty Sabo
Janet Sale
Georgia Smith
Marie Ethel Smith
Paticia Tait
Elizabeth Thompson
Jotina Trussell
Louise Turner
Sandy Tybor
Jacqueline Vodian
Melanie Wegner
Barbara Wright

Editor: Kathryn B. Godfrey

Appetizers and Beverages

WINTER'S LEAVING HOLY GHOST CREEK

In a narrow valley in the Sangre de Cristo Mountains rising north of Santa Fe, New Mexico, Holy Ghost Creek empties from Spirit Lake into the Pecos River as it flows toward Texas. The subtle color along the creek as the spring melt begins creates a palette of golds, bronzes and greens against the remaining snow. The creek is said to have been named by a priest who was concealed from the Pecos Indians by the mist which collects along the valley.

Baked Brie in Puff Pastry

Serves 8

1 8-oz. baby Brie
1 sheet Pepperidge Farm
    Puff Pastry

Preheat oven to 400°. Roll out pastry to ⅛-inch. Place Brie in center of pastry and wrap dough over cheese, sealing completely by crimping edges. Place on cookie sheet and bake for 15 minutes or until pastry is golden. Let stand 20 minutes before serving.

Dried Beef Cheese Ball

Serves 8

1 8-oz. package cream
    cheese
1 3-oz. jar dried beef
2 tsp. horseradish
2 tsp. minced onion
    diced parsley
    chopped nuts

Mix all ingredients. Roll into a ball and roll in nuts and parsley. Store in refrigerator until ready to serve.

Chile Cheese Squares

Yields 117 appetizers

2 lb. (8 cups) grated
    Cheddar cheese
1 lb. canned diced green
    chile
1 dozen eggs, well beaten
    paprika

Sprinkle half of cheese in well greased 9 x 13-inch baking pan, top with half of chile. Repeat layers. Pour eggs over all. Dust with paprika. Bake at 350° for 45 minutes. Cut into squares.
Note: Freezes well.

Chile Cheese Puff

Serves 8

1 sheet Pepperidge Farm Puff Pastry
1 lb. (4 cups) grated Cheddar cheese
1 4-oz. can diced green chile

Preheat oven to 425°. Roll pastry ⅛ inch thick. Top with cheese and chile. Fold pastry over and seal by crimping edges. Place on baking sheet. Bake for 25 minutes or until puffed and golden.
Note: Freezes well before or after baking.

Crabmeat Appetizer

Serves 32

1 7-oz. can crabmeat
½ cup margarine or butter, softened
1 5-oz. jar Old English cheese spread
1½ tsp. mayonnaise
½ tsp. garlic salt
½ tsp. seasoning salt
8 English muffins

Rinse crabmeat in cold water and drain well. Blend all ingredients and spread onto muffins. Let stand for 5 to 10 minutes. Put under preheated broiler until topping bubbles and muffins start to brown, about 3 minutes. Cut into bite-sized pieces to serve.
Note: Freezes well. Good as a light lunch, or with soup for supper.

Quick Garlic Bagel Thins

Serves 15

½ cup butter
8 cloves garlic, minced
2 T. lemon juice
½ tsp. salt
6 bagels, thinly sliced

Melt butter with garlic until garlic is soft, about 2 minutes. Add lemon juice and salt to taste. Brush bagel thins on one side with butter and broil until golden. These keep for a day in a tightly closed container.

Crab Mousse

Yields 1 quart

1 10-oz. can golden mushroom soup
1 8-oz. package cream cheese, softened
1 T. unflavored gelatin
3 T. water
1 6 to 7-oz. can crab meat
1 cup diced celery
2 green onions, chopped
1 cup mayonnaise

Heat soup and dissolve cheese in it. Dissolve gelatin in water. Combine all ingredients. Mix well and pour into 4 to 5 cup mold. Refrigerate at least 8 hours, covered. Unmold. Serve with crackers. *Note: This can be made a day ahead for a party.*

Crab with Prosciutto

Serves 18 to 24

24 thin slices prosciutto
12 oz. fresh crab
¼ cup butter
1 tsp. Worcestershire sauce
½ tsp. Tabasco
2 T. lemon juice
2 T. minced parsley
   black pepper

Place tsp. of crab on each slice of prosciutto. Wrap prosciutto around crab, cigar style. (This may be done early and refrigerated, or frozen.) Heat butter in skillet and add crab rolls. Cook until rolls fizzle and crab is hot. Add Worcestershire, Tabasco and lemon juice; heat. Garnish with parsley and pepper. Serve with toast points.

Green Spinach Dip

Yields 3 cups

1 cup sour cream
1 cup mayonnaise
1 10-oz. frozen package chopped spinach, thawed
1 oz. dry vegetable soup mix

Put all ingredients in blender and mix until blended. Refrigerate overnight. *Note: This instant GREEN dip can be made ahead. Perfect for parties, especially Christmas and St. Patrick's day.*

Effortless Appetizer

Yields 1½ lb.

1 lb. cream cheese,
       softened
½ lb. smoked or kippered
       salmon (not Lox)
2 T. minced dry onions
1 tsp. Worcestershire
       sauce
1 T. olive oil
       mushrooms
       paprika

Mix cheese, salmon, onions, Worcestershire and oil. Stuff mushrooms with filling and sprinkle with paprika.

Note: Tasty with bagels. May be cut in bite-size pieces and served as hors d'oeuvres, or as a bagel sandwich. Filling freezes well.

Fiesta Cheese Balls

Yields 16 logs or balls

2 lb. American cheese
3 lb. cheese spread
30 oz. sharp Cheddar
       cheese
20 oz. mild Cheddar cheese
2 lb. cream cheese
4 oz. bleu cheese
2 tsp. onion juice
2 tsp. garlic juice
1 T. Worcestershire sauce
       parsley and nuts

Put all cheeses through food processor and mix well. Add onion and garlic juice, and Worcestershire sauce. Mold into balls or rolls. Sprinkle with mixture of dried parsley and nuts. Refrigerate.

Note: Great for parties. Freezes well.

Lox Spread

Yields 1½ cups

1 8-oz. package cream
       cheese, room
       temperature
1 T. sour cream
1 3-oz. package of lox,
       diced, including oil
2 T. grated onion
       dash pepper

Mix all ingredients. Serve with rye crackers, rye cocktail bread, or on bagels.

Note: Freezes well. This is expensive, but a little goes a long way. Lox Spread is a special hors d'oeuvre or delicious sandwich.

Guacamole Albuquerque Style

Yields 1½ cups

2 ripe avocados, peeled, pitted and mashed
2 T. lemon juice
1 tomato, diced
3 green onions, thinly sliced
1 4-oz. can diced green chile
⅛ tsp. minced garlic
½ tsp. garlic salt

Combine all ingredients several hours before serving to allow flavors to blend. Store covered in refrigerator. *Note: Guacamole is a versatile New Mexico dish. It is served as an hors d'oeuvre with tortilla chips, as a salad in lettuce cups topped with tomatoes, ripe olives and tortilla chips, or as a topping for flautas, enchiladas, etc.*

Layered Shrimp

Serves 16

2 8-oz. packages cream cheese
2 T. Worcestershire sauce
1 T. lemon juice
½ cup thinly sliced green onion
⅛ tsp. Tabasco
1 12-oz. bottle tomato-based chile sauce
1 T. horseradish
¾ lb. small cooked shrimp assorted crackers

Beat cream cheese, Worcestershire, lemon juice, onions and Tabasco until smooth. Spread on a 10 to 12-inch rimmed serving plate, or pie plate. Stir together the chile sauce and horseradish. Spread over cheese mixture. Top with the shrimp. Serve with crackers. *Note: This great appetizer can be made several hours ahead and refrigerated until serving.*

Italian Dip

Yields 2 cups

2 cups plain yogurt
1 0.7-oz, envelope Italian salad dressing mix

Mix and chill. Serve with vegetable sticks.

Chile Cheese Dip

Yields 2 cups

⅛ cup minced dried
    onions
1 4-oz. can diced green
    chile
⅛ tsp. garlic powder
½ cup evaporated milk
1 8-oz. package process
    cheese spread, cubed
1 cup grated Cheddar
    cheese
    tortilla chips

Combine all ingredients in pan. Heat, stirring occasionally, until cheeses melt. Serve warm in chafing dish, with chips.

Party Puffs

Yields 48

1 envelope dry onion soup
    mix
1 lb. ground beef
1 cup shredded Cheddar
    cheese
3 packages refrigerator
    rolls

Preheat oven to 375°. In skillet combine soup mix and meat; brown well. Blend in cheese. Separate dough, cut in half and flatten slightly. Place spoon of meat on each piece of dough. Wrap and seal edges. Place on ungreased cookie sheet; bake 15 minutes or until golden.
Note: Freezes well. Ground turkey may be substituted.

Ultimate Cheese Ring

Yields 1 ring

1 lb. sharp Chedder
    cheese, grated
1 cup chopped nuts
1 cup mayonnaise
¼ cup grated onion
    black pepper

Combine all ingredients, mixing well. Pack into 5-cup ring mold and chill until firm. Remove ring from mold onto plate and fill center with strawberry preserves.

Pot Stickers

Yields 60

½ lb. ground beef or pork
1 8-oz. can water
  chestnuts, drained
  and minced
¼ cup soy sauce
8 green onions, chopped,
  white part only
2 garlic cloves, minced
½ tsp. chopped ginger
1 cup chopped Chinese
  cabbage
60 won ton wrappers

Combine all ingredients, except wrappers. This can be done 1 day ahead. Dust large baking sheet with flour. Place 2 tsp. of filling in center of wrapper. Brush edge with water. Fold wrapper over filling to form triangle. Pleat edges to form half-moon shape; press to seal. Arrange on baking sheet, pleated side up. Repeat with remaining filling and wrappers. (Can be prepared 4 hours ahead to this point. Cover and refrigerate.) Heat 1 T. oil in skillet. Stand as many pot stickers in pan as will fit in single layer. Cook until bottoms are crisp and brown, about 5 minutes. Add enough water to just cover bottom of pan. Cover pan and steam pot stickers 8 minutes or until cooked through. Transfer to warm plate. Repeat with remaining pot stickers. Serve immediately, passing sauce separately, or freeze.
Sauce: Combine ¼ cup soy sauce and ⅛ cup rice vinegar.
Note: Microwave frozen pot stickers to serve.

New Mexico Cheese Blintzes Yields 4 dozen

1½ lb. loaf white bread,
crusts removed
1 8-oz. package cream
cheese, softened
1 egg yolk
¼ cup sugar
½ cup butter or margarine
1 small onion, minced
¼ cup green chile,
chopped
paprika

Beat cheese, yolk and sugar. Add onion and chile. Roll bread paper-thin with rolling pin. Place 1 T. cream cheese mixture on each slice, spread, roll up jelly roll style and cut in half. Roll in melted butter until coated. Place on waxed paper, seam side down, for half hour to absorb butter. Can be refrigerated or frozen at this point. Bake at 400° for 15 minutes or until golden. Sprinkle with paprika and serve warm.

Reuben Dip Serves 8 to 10

1 12-oz. can corned beef
1 1-lb. can sauerkraut
1 T. caraway seed
3 T. mayonnaise
2 T. dark mustard
2 tsp. horseradish
8 oz. Swiss cheese, cubed

Preheat oven to 350°. Mix all ingredients except cheese. Place in 1 quart casserole, top with cheese and bake for 30 minutes. Serve warm with cocktail rye bread or crackers. *Note: If you like Reuben sandwiches you'll love this. It can be frozen before or after baking.*

Rye Spread

Yields 1 quart

1⅓ cups sour cream
1⅓ cups mayonnaise
6 oz. chopped corned beef
2 T. minced onion
2 T. chopped fresh
    parsley
2 tsp. dill seed
1 to 2 tsp. Beau Monde
    seasoning
1 small cocktail rye loaf

Combine all ingredients except bread. Cover and refrigerate overnight. Serve with rye slices.

New Mexico Layered Ranchero Dip

Serves 12

1 15-oz. can refried beans
4 oz. sour cream
⅓ cup mayonnaise
2 avocados, pitted and
    peeled
1 4-oz. can diced green
    chile
1 tomato, chopped
2 green onions, chopped
2 T. lemon juice
1 tsp. garlic salt
1 8-oz. jar taco or picante
    sauce
1 cup shredded cheddar
    cheese
  tortilla chips

Blend beans, sour cream and mayonnaise. Spread in bottom of 10 inch plate with 1 inch sides. Mash ripe avocados, add chile, tomato, onion, lemon juice and garlic salt. Blend thoroughly and top bean mixture. Top this layer with taco sauce, and top all with cheese. Serve chilled with tortilla chips.

Siu Mai (Dim Sum)
Yields 24 to 30

8 oz. uncooked, peeled
    medium shrimp,
    chopped
1 lb. uncooked lean
    ground pork
¼ head small cabbage,
    chopped
6 green onions, chopped
4 dried mushrooms,
    soaked and chopped
2 eggs, lightly beaten
3 to 4 T. flour
¼ cup plus 1 T. soy sauce
1 T. oyster sauce
1 T. sesame oil
24-30 won ton wrappers
⅛ cup lemon juice

Mix shrimp, pork, cabbage, onion, mushrooms, eggs, flour 1 T. soy sauce, oyster sauce and sesame oil until well combined. Place 1 T. of mixture onto center of each won ton wrapper. Gently press wrappers around filling, tucking edges together but leaving tops open. Steam Siu Mai for 30 minutes. Combine ¼ cup soy sauce and lemon. Serve Siu Mai warm or cold with soy and lemon mixture for dipping.
Note: Freezes well. Reheat in microwave.

Zippy Mushroom Appetizers
Serves 8

⅔ cup tarragon vinegar
½ cup salad oil
1 clove garlic, minced
1 T. sugar
1½ tsp. salt
    dash pepper
2 T. water
    dash Tabasco
1 medium onion sliced
    and separated in
    rings
2 pints fresh mushrooms,
    cleaned

Combine first 8 ingredients. Add onions and mushrooms. Cover and refrigerate mixture for at least 8 hours, stirring several times. Drain and serve as an appetizer.
Note: Not only are these made ahead, but they are yummy, quick and easy!

Parmechoke Dip

Yields 1 quart

1 cup mayonnaise
1 7-oz. can diced chile, undrained
8 oz. drained artichoke hearts, chopped
1 cup Parmesan cheese, grated

Preheat oven to 350°. Combine all ingredients, turn into an 8-inch baking dish. Bake about 20 minutes or until heated through.

Note: Serve warm with corn tortilla chips or crackers. A quick, delicious appetizer!

Six Minute Microwave Salty Bridge Mix

Yields 1 gallon

8 cups mixed cereals and pretzels
8 oz. peanuts
¾ cup butter or margarine
2 T. Worcestershire sauce
1 tsp. garlic salt

In microwave melt butter and add seasonings. Pour cereals, pretzels and nuts in 9 x 13 inch glass pan. Pour butter over cereal mix. Stir to coat. Cook on high for 6 minutes. Stir every 2 minutes. Cool. Store in airtight container.

Won Ton Crispies

Yields 40

20 won ton skins
4 T. butter or margarine
8 T. Parmesan cheese

Preheat oven to 375°. Place won ton skins on cookie sheets and spread with melted butter. Cut in half to form rectangles. Sprinkle tops with grated Parmesan. Bake uncovered in oven for 5 to 6 minutes or until golden.

Variation: For sweet crackers, combine ¼ cup sugar and 1 tsp. cinnamon. Substitute sugar mixture for Parmesan.

Teriyaki Meatballs

Yields 100 meatballs

2 lb. lean ground beef or
   turkey
½ cup bread crumbs
½ cup milk
2 eggs
1 tsp. salt
½ tsp. garlic salt
2 T. cornstarch
⅓ cup soy sauce
¼ cup sugar
1 clove garlic, minced
2 tsp. minced fresh ginger
   or ½ tsp. ground
2¼ cups chicken broth

Combine the meat, crumbs, milk, eggs and salts in bowl. Mix to blend. Shape into balls about the size of large marbles and arrange in shallow baking pans. Put into 500 degree oven for 4 to 5 minutes or until lightly browned. In a pan, blend together cornstarch, soy sauce, sugar, garlic, ginger and broth. Cook, stirring until blended and thickened. Pour over meatballs in pan, refrigerate, then reheat at serving time. *Note: Serve in chafing dish over candle. This do-ahead party food is a sure winner.*

Puffed Cheese and Salami Rolls Yields 16

1 sheet Pepperidge Farm
   Puff Pastry
4 oz. thin-sliced hard
   salami
2 slices Swiss cheese
8 pitted black olives,
   halved
1 egg beaten with
1 tsp. of water

Preheat oven to 400°. Roll pastry to ⅛-inch thickness. Arrange salami, cheese and olives evenly over pastry and roll up jelly roll style. Seal and place on baking sheet seam side down. Cut slices in roll about ¼ inch wide, but keep roll intact. Bake for 10 minutes or until puffed and golden. Serve warm.
Note: Quick, easy appetizer.

Mushroom Roll-ups Albuquerque Style

Yields 75

1 large onion, minced
1½ cup minced fresh
   mushrooms
3 T. butter
1 4-oz. can diced green
   chile
2 T. flour
½ tsp. basil
½ tsp. salt
½ cup sour cream
1 loaf sliced sandwich
   bread

Preheat oven to 400°. Saute onions and mushrooms in butter. Add flour, seasonings, chile and sour cream. Heat but do not boil. Mix and cool. Cut crusts from bread. Roll bread slices flat with rolling-pin and spread with filling. Roll up jelly roll style, brush with melted butter, cut in thirds and bake for 10 minutes or until brown.

Note: Freezes well before or after baking. Serve warm or at room temperature.

Reuben Puffs

Serves 8

1 sheet Pepperidge Farm
   Puff Pastry, thawed
½ lb. corned beef, sliced
   thin
¼ lb. Swiss cheese, sliced
1 cup well drained
   sauerkraut
½ cup French Dressing

Preheat oven to 400°. Roll pastry out to 8 x 12-inches. Layer with corned beef, cheese, sauerkraut, and top with French dressing. Fold pastry in half and seal edges. Bake for 20 minutes at 400°, then reduce heat to 350° and bake about another 30 minutes or until golden. Slice and serve.

Pesto Torta

Serves 20

1   lb. cream cheese
1   lb. butter
2½ cups fresh basil leaves,
        or ½ cup dry basil
1   cup Parmesan cheese
⅓   cup olive oil
¼   cup pine nuts

Beat cream cheese and butter until smooth. Make pesto in blender or food processor by blending basil, Parmesan cheese and oil to a paste. Stir in nuts. Line straight-sided mold, loaf pan, or flower pot with plastic wrap. Cover bottom with 1/6 of cheese. Next, cover with 1/5 of pesto, extending it evenly to sides of the mold. Repeat layers using remaining cheese and pesto, ending with cheese. Fold ends of wrap over torta and press down lightly to compact. Chill 1 hour until firm. Invert onto platter and remove wrap. Serve with bread or crackers. *Note: This looks complicated but is easy to make. It keeps a week in refrigerator and freezes well. It can be made in small molds and defrosted as needed.*

Shrimp Mold

Serves 12

1   10-oz. can tomato soup
1   8-oz. package cream
        cheese
1½ T. unflavored gelatin
¼   cup water
¾   cup chopped onion
¾   cup chopped celery
1   4-oz. can shrimp
1   cup mayonnaise

Grease a 1-quart mold with mayonnaise. Heat soup to boiling, add cheese and melt. Dissolve gelatin in water and mix thoroughly with soup mixture. Cool slightly. Add remaining ingredients. Pour into mold. Chill. Serve with crackers.

Great Grapes

Serves 8

1½ lb. seedless grapes
1 cup sour cream
1 tsp. vanilla
1 cup dark brown sugar

Wash grapes, but leave clusters intact; chill. Combine sour cream and vanilla in bowl. Arrange grapes on platter with separate bowls of cream and sugar alongside. Dip grapes in cream, then in sugar. So refreshing on a hot summer evening!

Pate

Yields 2 cups

1 10½-oz. can consomme, undiluted
1 envelope unflavored gelatin
6 oz. Braunschweiger
1 T. grated onion
2 T. Miracle Whip
3-4 drops Tabasco

Dissolve gelatin in consomme. Soften and pour ⅓ into mold; refrigerate. Blend other ingredients with remaining gelatin-consomme mixture. When first ⅓ has set, add balance. (Rake top with fork before adding last ⅔.)
Note: Keeps several days in refrigerator. Delicious served with crackers.

Seasoned Oyster Crackers

Yields 1 gallon

24 oz. Oyster Crackers
½ cup butter flavored popcorn oil
1 tsp. dill weed
1 tsp. lemon pepper
1 2-oz. package dry original Ranch Dressing mix

Place crackers into bowl. Combine oil and dry seasonings, mix well. Pour over crackers, toss to coat.
Note: These tasty crackers are good on salads, in soups or just as a snack. They store covered at room temperature.

Artichoke Squares   Yields 12

3   green onions, sliced
1   T. butter or margarine
2   6-oz. jars marinated
      artichoke hearts,
      drained and chopped
1   cup mayonnaise
1   T. chopped parsley
1   garlic clove, minced
2   cups grated Cheddar
      cheese
6   soda crackers, crushed
4   eggs, beaten
    dash Tabasco
    salt and pepper to taste

Preheat oven to 350°. Grease a 1 quart baking dish. Saute onions in butter. Add remaining ingredients and beat well. Pour into baking dish and bake for 30 minutes or until done. Cut and serve.
Note: Recipe can be doubled.

Sausage Appetizers   Yields 48

1   8-oz. package
      refrigerator
      butterflake rolls
½   lb. hot sausage,
      crumbled
2   eggs, beaten
1   cup cottage cheese
1   T. snipped chives
    dash pepper
¼   cup Parmesan cheese

Preheat oven to 375°. Generously grease miniature muffin tins. Separate rolls into 8 sections each. Press into muffin cups. Brown sausage and drain. Spoon equally over dough. Mix eggs, cottage cheese, chives and pepper. Stir in Parmesan. Spoon over sausage and bake 20 minutes or until golden.
Note: Can be made ahead and frozen before or after baking. Reheat in microwave oven.

Simple Baked Mushrooms   Serves 36

36 Mushrooms
    Seasoned Salt

Preheat oven to 350°. Clean mushrooms and place on baking plate. Sprinkle with seasoned salt as you would salt a steak. Bake 10 minutes until warm. Serve warm.
Note: Simple, but tasty.

Cherry Tomatoes with Salmon Pate
Yields 6 dozen

1 15-oz. can salmon,
   drained
6 oz. cream cheese
3 T. horseradish
2 green onions
1 T. parsley
1 T. lemon juice
2 drops Tabasco
⅛ tsp. Worcestershire
   sauce
3 pints cherry tomatoes

Remove skin and bones from salmon. Place all ingredients, except tomatoes, in food processor and process until smooth. Chill overnight. Cut tops off tomatoes, hollow out pulp (small melon scoop works well), invert to drain. With star tip on pastry bag, fill tomatoes. Garnish with additional parsley if desired.

Shanghai Chicken Wings   Yields 12

12 chicken wings
⅓ cup soy sauce
2 T. sugar
1 T. dry Sherry wine
2 slices ginger root
⅓ cup water

The day before serving, combine all ingredients in pan. Cover and simmer for 20 minutes, stirring occasionally. Uncover and simmer another 15 minutes until ½ cup liquid remains. Cover and refrigerate. Serve cold.

Chinese Water Chestnuts   Yields 24

1 8-oz. can water
   chestnuts, drained
2 T. brown sugar
8 slices bacon, cut in
   thirds

Preheat oven to 425°. Combine water chestnuts and sugar. Wrap bacon around water chestnuts and secure with toothpick. Place in baking dish. Bake for 15 minutes or until bacon is golden. Serve hot.

Jicama Fresca   Yields 4 dozen

1 T. salt
½ tsp. chili powder
2 lbs. jicama, peeled and
   sliced
1 lime, thinly sliced

Combine salt and chili powder. Place jicama on serving platter. Top with lime and salt mixture. Serve chilled or at room temperature.
Note: Good served with Margaritas

Imperial Cocktail Meatballs   Yields 100

½ lb. ground smoked ham
¾ lb. ground beef
½ lb. ground pork
1 cup milk
2 cups wheat flakes,
   crushed
2 eggs, beaten
1 tsp. salt
1¼ cups brown sugar
½ cup cider vinegar
1 cup water
1 tsp. dry mustard

Combine ham, beef, pork, milk, flakes, eggs and salt. Shape into small balls. Preheat oven to 350°. Combine sugar, vinegar, water and mustard. Pour over meatballs and bake for 1¼ hours.
Note: Freezes well.

Meat and Cheese Squares   Yields 12

1 2½-oz. package wafer-
   thin beef
1 3-oz. package cream
   cheese, cut in 12
   cubes

Place 1 cube of cheese in center of each beef slice, fold, and secure with toothpick. Refrigerate until serving.
Note: It's surprising that something so simple can taste so good.

Meat Treat   Yields 100

1 lb. ground beef
1 lb. hot sausage
1 lb. process cheese

In skillet cook meats and drain. Add cheese and cook over low heat until melted. Spread on cocktail rye bread or crackers.
Note: Freezes well.

Prosciutto Breadsticks   Serves 12

12 thin slices prosciutto
12 Italian breadsticks

Wrap prosciutto (cigar-style) evenly around upper half of breadstick only. Place in vase or other narrow container, meat end up, cover and refrigerate until serving.
Note: These add a nice vertical line to an appetizer tray and are great with any of the summer melons.

Ranchero Dip

Yields 1½ cups

⅔ cup mayonnaise
⅔ cup sour cream
2 tsp. chopped parsley
1 tsp. Beau Monde
1 tsp. dill weed
1 1-oz. package Hidden
   Ranch Valley Salad
   Dressing Mix, orig-
   inal flavor, dry

Combine all ingredients and chill.

Note: This quick, easy dip is good as an hors d'oeuvre with vegetables or chips. It is also good served on baked potatoes.

Sausage Delight

Yields 5 dozen

1 lb. hot sausage, cooked
2 cups grated sharp
   Cheddar cheese
3 cups biscuit mix

Preheat oven to 350°. Combine all ingredients and roll tablespoons of dough into balls. Freeze or refrigerate until ready to use. Bake in shallow pan for 15 minutes or until golden.

Shrimp on The Half Shell

Serves 8

1 lb. jumbo shrimp
3 T. oil
1 clove garlic, minced
1 tsp. fresh ginger,
   minced
3 T. scallions, minced
2 T. soy sauce
2 T. whisky
¼ cup chicken broth

Split shrimp in half lengthwise, shell and all. Remove veins, but leave shrimp in halved shells. Heat oil in heavy skillet or chafing dish. Arrange shrimp, shell side down, in the pan and cook gently for 5 minutes. Add remaining ingredients. Cover and simmer until done, 5 to 10 minutes.

SOUTHWEST SEASONS SOUTHWEST SEASON: SOUTHWEST SEASONS SOUTHWEST SEASONS SOUTHWEST

Advanced Margarita   Serves 8

1 12-oz. can limeade
12 liquid oz. sweet and
       sour bar mix
8 oz. tequila
4 oz. triple sec

Place all ingredients in blender and fill with ice. Blend and serve or freeze.

Note: This Margarita may be made in advance and held in the freezer, covered, for several months.

Albuquerque Pina Colada   Serves 8

1 cup rum
7 oz. cream of coconut
1 8-oz. can crushed
       pineapple, undrained
   ice

Combine all ingredients in blender, fill with ice. Blend until smooth. Serve immediately.

Note: Most refreshing!
Variation: For ChiChi, substitute vodka for rum.

Egg Nog   Yields 3 quarts

8 eggs
½ pint whipping cream
1 quart half-and-half
½ cup sugar
1 tsp. vanilla
1½ cups brandy
   whole milk
   nutmeg

Put eggs, cream, sugar and vanilla in blender. Blend 1 minute. Pour into 2½-quart container. Add half and half and fill to top with whole milk. Refrigerate. When ready to serve, add brandy, mix, top with nutmeg. Serve.

Note: The Holidays are hardly complete without egg nog. Recipe can be doubled.

Homemade Coffee Liqueur Yields 1½ quarts

1   cup water
3   cups sugar
12 T. instant coffee
3   T. vanilla
1   quart vodka

Boil water, sugar and coffee for 15 minutes. Cool. Add vanilla and vodka. Serve over crushed ice.

Hot Buttered Rum   Serves 24

½   cup butter
1   lb. brown sugar
¼   tsp. nutmeg
¼   tsp. cinnamon
¼   tsp. cloves
    rum
    cinnamon stick

Cream butter, sugar and spices; refrigerate. To make drink, place 1 T. of mixture and 1½ oz. of rum in mug and fill with boiling water. Stir, garnish with cinnamon stick to serve.
Note: Mixture keeps in refrigerator for a month, but may also be frozen. This is a great drink after skiing.

Hot Mulled Cider   Serves 10

½   cup brown sugar
¼   tsp. salt
2   quarts cider
1   tsp. whole allspice
1   tsp. whole cloves
1   3-inch stick cinnamon

Combine brown sugar, salt and cider. Tie spices in small piece of cheesecloth; add to cider mixture. Slowly bring to boiling; simmer, covered, 20 minutes. Remove spices. Serve hot. Float clove-studded orange slices atop.

Iced Lemon-Mint Tea

Yields 2 gallons

6 tea bags
¼ cup loosely packed fresh
   mint
4 12-oz. cans frozen
   lemonade
   concentrate

Brew tea: Boil 1 quart of water. Add tea bags and mint leaves. Steep uncovered for 5 minutes. Discard tea and mint. Add lemonade and enough water to yield 2 gallons. Serve over ice. Garnish with lemon slices and mint sprigs if desired.

Note: This is ideal for parties as it can be made in advance and no additional sugar or spoons are required.

Liquid Cream

Serves 1

1 scoop vanilla ice cream
⅔ cup orange juice

In blender, blend ice cream and juice a few seconds. Serve immediately.

Note: Recipe may be doubled or tripled. Refreshing!

Liquid Sunshine

Serves 4

1 6-oz. can orange juice
   concentrate
1½ T. vanilla pudding mix,
   NOT instant
4 T. sugar
1 cup water
   ice

Put all ingredients in blender, fill with ice and blend. Serve immediately.

Note: Few drinks are more refreshing than this on a hot summer day. Children of all ages will ask for seconds.

Slush   **Serves 16**

8   cups boiling water
1   cup sugar
1   12-oz. can lemonade
1   12-oz. can orange juice
1   cup whiskey

Stir water and sugar until sugar is dissolved. Add remaining ingredients, mix well and freeze. Serve in glass with ice tea spoon.

Note: This is simple to make ahead and is a very refreshing summer drink.

Strawberry Daiquiri   **Serves 6**

8   oz. light rum
1   6-oz. can lemonade
1   10-oz. package frozen
      strawberries

Put all in blender, fill with ice, blend and serve.

Note: This is a pretty drink and very refreshing in the summer.

Sunshine Punch   **Yields 1 gallon**

1   46-oz. can pineapple
      juice
1   14-oz. can sweetened
      condensed milk
1   6-oz. can frozen orange
      juice concentrate,
      thawed
2   32-oz. bottles
      lemon/lime soda

In punch bowl combine all ingredients except soda. Just before serving add soda, mix to blend. Garnish with orange sherbet, orange slices and mint, if desired.

Note: Recipe can be doubled. This is so good you'd best get ready to serve lots of second helpings.

Tom and Jerry's

Serves 35

12　eggs, separated
⅛　tsp. cream of tartar
2　lb. plus 1½ cups
　　powdered sugar,
　　divided
3　T. lemon juice
　　brandy
　　rum
　　nutmeg

Beat egg whites with cream of tartar for 10 minutes. Beat in 1½ cups powdered sugar. Set aside. Beat yolks with lemon juice for 15 minutes. Add 2 lb. powdered sugar. Beat until very thick. Fold in whites. Store refrigerated in an air-tight container. To serve, place ½ jigger each rum and brandy in a large warmed mug. Fill ⅓ full with batter. Add boiling water to fill. Sprinkle with nutmeg. Sip, don't stir.

Note: Batter will keep throughout the Holiday Season.

Wedding Punch

Yields 36 cups of concentrate

1　6-oz. box orange gelatin
1　6-oz. box strawberry
　　gelatin
4　cups hot water
3　cups sugar
2　cups cold water
2　46-oz. cans pineapple
　　juice
2　46-oz. cans orange juice
2　12-oz. cans frozen
　　lemonade
　　lemon-lime soda

Mix together the orange and strawberry gelatin, hot water and sugar, until dissolved. Add the cold water, fruit juices and lemonade, mix well. Freeze in 3 large zip lock bags (approximately 12 cups per bag). When ready to serve, add 2 quarts soda for each bag.

Note: Having the punch all ready except to add the soda makes this an ideal cooler for big crowds.

Fun on the Beach   **Serves 1**

1 12-oz. glass, filled with
    ice
½ tsp. Grenadine
1 oz. coconut-flavor rum
⅓ cup pineapple juice
⅓ cup cola
1 T. whipping cream

In glass combine all ingredients; stir well.
Note: Very refreshing.

Krupnikas   **Yields 2 quarts**

10 cloves
10 whole allspice
3 sticks cinnamon
1 stick vanilla
2 slices ginger
10 cardamom seeds
½ nutmeg
½ tsp. orange rind
½ tsp. lemon rind
⅛ tsp. saffron
4 cups water
2 lbs. honey
1 quart 190-proof grain
    alcohol

Warning: Alcohol is highly flammable.

Boil spices, rinds and water in covered pot for 1 hour or until liquid is reduced to 2 cups. Strain. Bring honey to boil, skimming off foam. Pour water mixture into honey. Remove from heat and carefully pour into alcohol. Return to low heat for 15 minutes. (Do not simmer or boil.) Cool. Strain through cloth or paper. Store in bottles.
Note: This Lithuanian Honey Liqueur often is served warm in the winter.

Soups, Salads, and Sandwiches

PEACH BLOSSOMS

Seama, one of a group of small villages which form Laguna Pueblo, means *door* or *gate* in the Keres-Laguna language. Located west of Albuquerque on the road to Gallup, New Mexico, it is a natural gateway to the Canada de la Cruz, a wide valley of the Rio San Jose. The flowering fruit trees are splashes of beautiful color on the otherwise austere landscape.

Big A's Black Bean Soup

Serves 6

1 cup dry black beans
6 cups beef broth
¾ cup olive oil
1 cup chopped celery
1 cup chopped onion
2 cloves garlic, minced
½ cup uncooked rice
⅛ tsp. cayenne
1 whole bay leaf
1 tsp. salt
4 peppercorns
2 whole cloves

Cover cleaned beans with water and soak overnight. Drain and cook 2 hours in broth. Heat oil and saute celery, onion and garlic until tender. Combine all ingredients and cook for 2 hours. Stir occasionally.
Note: Freezes well. Can be doubled.

Chilled Cherry-Champagne Soup

Serves 6 to 8

2 16-oz. packages frozen pie cherries
1 T. grated orange rind
½ tsp. cinnamon
2 T. cornstarch
3 T. water
1 cup of sugar or to taste
½ cup orange liqueur
1 750-ml bottle of champagne, chilled

In a large saucepan, heat cherries. Dissolve cornstarch in water. Add sugar, rind, cinnamon and cornstarch mixture to cherries. Cook until thickened. Remove from heat and stir in liqueur. Cover and chill. This may be done several days in advance. When ready to serve, add champagne and ladle into chilled soup bowls.

Cucumber Soup

Serves 6

3 medium cucumbers, peeled and diced
3 cups chicken broth
1½ cups sour cream
1½ cups whipping cream
3 T. white vinegar
2 tsp. garlic salt
2 tomatoes, peeled and chopped
½ cup sliced green onions
¾ cup toasted almonds
½ cup chopped parsley

Puree cucumbers with broth. Combine creams, vinegar and garlic salt. Stir just to mix. Pour into bowls. Sprinkle with tomatoes, almonds, onions and parsley.

Note: This cool summer soup will keep several days in the refrigerator or can be frozen.

Gazpacho

Yields 6 cups

1 cup peeled tomatoes
½ cup diced green chile
½ cup chopped celery
½ cup chopped cucumber
¼ cup chopped onion
2 tsp. chopped parsley
1 tsp. chopped chives
1 clove garlic, chopped
3 T. wine vinegar
2 T. oil
1 tsp. salt
½ tsp. black pepper
½ tsp. Worcestershire sauce
4 cups tomato juice

Place all vegetables in blender and blend well. In bowl, combine vegetables and remaining ingredients. Store in refrigerator 24 hours before serving. Serve cold.

Note: Freezes well. Gazpacho is a cold, refreshing, spicy soup that is very popular in the Southwest. It is made ahead and is ideal for a summer party. This was served at the Governor's Mansion in Santa Fe, New Mexico in 1977 to the Casa Angelica Auxiliary.

Lemon Mint Summer Soup   Serves 4 to 5

1 10¾-oz. can cream of
   chicken soup
1 10¾-oz. can chicken
   broth
4 T. lemon juice
¼ tsp. lemon rind
5 fresh whole mint leaves,
   or 1 tsp. dried mint
4 or 5 thin lemon slices
   salt to taste
   dash Tabasco

Combine all ingredients in blender except lemon slices and whole mint leaves. Blend until mixture is smooth. Chill in refrigerator. Float lemon slice topped with fresh mint leaf on each portion.

Note: Recipe can be doubled. Great for a hot summer day. Served warmed, it also has a nice flavor for the fall.

Mexican Chili Con Queso Soup

Serves 4 to 6

3 T. butter
1 large onion, minced
1 28-oz. can peeled
   tomatoes, diced,
   reserve liquid
1 4-oz. can diced green
   chile
1 2-oz. jar pimentos,
   diced
   salt and pepper to taste
½ lb. cheddar cheese,
   grated
¼ lb. Monterey Jack
   cheese, grated

Combine butter and onion in 2 quart microwave safe container. Cover and micro-wave on high 7 minutes, stirring once. Add tomatoes and liquid, chile, pimentos, salt and pepper and blend well. Cover and microwave on high until mixture comes to a full boil, about 9 to 10 minutes. Stir in cheeses. Continue cooking on high just until cheeses are melted, about 1 minute. Serve hot.

SOUTHWEST SEASONS SOUTHWEST SEASONS SOUTHWEST SEASONS SOUTHWEST SEASONS SOUTHWEST

New England Clam Chowder   Serves 12

5 10¾-oz. cans cream of
      potato soup
6 cups half-and-half
1 10-oz. can whole baby
      clams, undrained
1 T. dried minced onion
1 T. dried parsley flakes
½ tsp. garlic powder
½ tsp. seasoned salt
      salt and pepper to taste
¼ cup butter

Heat soup with half and half in large saucepan. Add clams, onion, parsley, garlic powder, seasoned salt and salt and pepper. Reduce heat to low. Simmer gently until thickened, stirring frequently, about 15 minutes. Serve topped with a pat of butter. *Note: Recipe can be doubled. Freezes well.*

Hot and Sour Soup   Serves 4

¼ cup pork, cooked and
      shredded
1 tsp. dry Sherry wine
3 T. cornstarch
1 14-oz. can chicken broth
1½ cups water
½ tsp. salt
1 T. soy sauce
¼ cup mushrooms, diced
½ cup bean curd,
      shredded
1 egg, beaten
3 T. cider vinegar
¼ tsp. white pepper
1 tsp. sesame seed oil
1 T. green onions, minced

Mix pork, sherry and 1 tsp. cornstarch. Mix the remaining cornstarch with ½ cup water. Put vinegar and pepper in serving bowl. Combine broth, water, salt and soy sauce in pan. Bring to boil. Stir in pork. Add bean curd and return to boil. Stir in cornstarch mixture until soup thickens. Mix in egg and remove from heat. Pour soup into the serving bowl with the vinegar and pepper. Garnish with oil and green onions. Serve hot.

New Mexican Soup

Serves 4

4   slices bacon, diced
¾   cup chopped onion
¾   cup chopped celery
½   cup diced green chile
1   clove garlic, minced
1   16-oz. can refried beans
¼   tsp. pepper
¼   tsp. chili powder
1   14½-oz. can chicken
      broth
    shredded Cheddar
      cheese
    crushed tortilla chips

In a 2 quart saucepan cook bacon until crisp. Do not drain. Add onion, celery, green chile and garlic; cook, covered over low heat, stirring occasionally, about 10 minutes or until vegetables are tender but not brown. Add beans, pepper and chili powder. Stir in chicken broth. Bring to boil. Serve topped with cheese and chips.

Note: This soup has the REAL flavor of New Mexico. Freezes well. Recipe can be doubled.

Nine Bean Crockpot Soup

Serves 8 to 10

2   cups nine bean soup
      mix
    water to cover
1   lb. ham, diced
1   large onion, chopped
1   clove garlic, minced
½   tsp. salt
1   large can tomatoes,
      diced, undrained
1   4-oz. can diced green
      chile

Soak soup mix overnight. Drain soup mix and put in crockpot. Add remaining ingredients and enough water to just cover beans. Cook in crockpot for 24 hours. Serve hot topped with grated cheddar cheese.

Note: Nine Bean Soup Mix consists of 1 lb. each: pinto beans, red beans, black beans, white beans, black-eyed peas, lentils, green split peas, yellow split peas and barley. Soup freezes well.

Roquefort Soup

Serves 8 to 10

½ cup butter
1 large head cabbage,
   chopped
1 medium head
   cauliflower, chopped
7 cups chicken broth
1 cup whipping cream
¼ cup Roquefort cheese
   buttered croutons

Melt butter in pan. Add cabbage. Stir to coat. Cook uncovered until soft, stirring occasionally. Add cauliflower and chicken broth. Bring to boil. Reduce heat, cover and simmer 30 minutes until vegetables are tender. Combine all ingredients, except croutons, in blender and blend until smooth. Reheat before serving and top with croutons.
Note: Freezes well.

Tortilla Soup

Serves 6

1 4-oz. can diced green
   chile
3 tomatoes, peeled and
   diced
1 medium onion, diced
1 clove garlic
2 T. oil
6 cups chicken broth
2 cups broken tortilla
   chips
2 cups shredded cheddar
   cheese

In blender container combine chile, tomato, onion and garlic; cover and blend until chopped. In 3 quart pan combine tomato mixture and oil. Cook, uncovered, 10 minutes. Add broth. Bring to boiling; cover and simmer 10 minutes. Stir in tortillas and cheese when serving.

Chilled Apricot Soup   Serves 6

1 lb. dried apricots
24 oz. whipping cream
½ cup sauterne
½ cup sour cream, divided
½ tsp. cinnamon
⅛ tsp. nutmeg
1 T. lemon juice
½ cup sugar
⅛ tsp. salt
1 tsp. grated orange rind
6 mint leaves

Soak apricots overnight in wine and whipping cream. The next day, puree apricot mixture in a blender or food processor. Reserving ¼ cup sour cream for garnish, add remaining ingredients to apricot mixture and puree again. Chill and scrve in chilled soup bowls with a garnish of sour cream, zest and mint leaves. For a thinner soup you may strain mixture after the second puree.

Chinese Egg Drop Soup   Serves 8

2 14-oz. cans chicken
   broth
1 quart water
2 tsp. salt
2 slices ginger root
1 tsp. dry Sherry wine
4 eggs, beaten
2 T. green onions, minced
4 T. cornstarch
1 cup water

Combine broth, 1 quart water, salt, and ginger. Combine eggs and sherry, and set aside. Combine cornstarch and 1 cup water and add to broth. Bring to a boil. Add egg mixture in a steady thin stream while stirring constantly. Garnish with green onions.

Avocados Vinaigarette   Serves 8

4 ripe avocados
1 T. balsamic vinegar
1 T. olive oil
   salt and pepper

Halve avocados lengthwise, remove pits; and place each half in lettuce lined goblet, cut side up. Combine vinegar and oil. Place ⅛ in each cavity. Sprinkle with salt and pepper to taste.

Bacon and Nut Salad   Serves 8

½ cup imitation bacon bits
¾ cup chopped walnuts
1 cup sour cream
2 T. lemon juice
2 tsp. sugar
   salt and pepper to taste
1 head lettuce

Combine nuts and bacon, set aside. Mix sour cream, lemon juice, sugar, salt and pepper. Shred lettuce, pour sour cream mixture over, and top with nut mixture.

B. O. B. Salad   Serves 12

1 large head of broccoli, florets only
1 onion, cut into rings
1 30-oz. can kidney beans, drained
1 lb. grated cheese
2 cups Italian dressing

Combine broccoli, onion, beans and cheese. Pour dressing over vegetables and cheese. Marinate at least 4 hours, or overnight.

BBC Salad

Serves 8

- 1 large head broccoli, cut into small florets
- ½ cup cooked crumbled bacon
- 1 cauliflower, cut into small florets
- 1 large tomato, chopped
- 1 small onion, chopped
- 2 hard-cooked eggs, chopped
- 1 cup Italian dressing
- ¼ cup seasoned breadcrumbs

Combine vegetables and eggs in a large bowl. Pour dressing over and toss. Sprinkle breadcrumbs over. Serve.

Note: This quick, easy salad can be made even easier when you use frozen broccoli and cauliflower (microwave until crisp tender and chill), and bacon bits.

Fruit and Greens Salad

Yields 1½ cups

- 1 tsp. dry mustard
- 1 tsp. salt
- ¼ cup sugar
- 2 tsp. grated onion
- 2 T. red wine vinegar
- ½ tsp. celery seed
- ½ tsp. paprika
- 1 cup salad oil
- 1 head lettuce
- 1 cup grapefruit or orange sections
- ½ red onion, sliced
- 2 avocados, diced

In blender combine mustard, salt, sugar, onion, vinegar, celery seed and paprika. Blend while adding oil slowly. Cover and refrigerate. Tear lettuce into bite-size pieces. To lettuce, add fruit sections, onion and avocados. Top with dressing and toss to coat.

Note: A great complement to any Southwestern entree.

Cinnamon Applesauce Salad   Serves 6

¼ cup red cinnamon
    candies
1 cup water
1 3-oz. package
    strawberry gelatin
    dash of salt
1½ cups sweetened
    applesauce, chilled

Melt candies in water over medium heat, stirring constantly. Remove from heat and dissolve gelatin and salt in hot liquid. Add applesauce and mix well. Pour into 1-quart mold and chill until firm. Unmold and serve.
Note: Children love this salad.

Confetti Corn Salad   Serves 6

1 16-oz. package frozen
    whole kernel corn
½ cup chopped green
    pepper
2 T. chopped red onion
1 T. snipped parsley
⅓ cup mayonnaise
2 T. sour cream
½ tsp. beef bouillon
1 T. red wine vinegar
¼ tsp. salt
    dash pepper
4 slices bacon

Cook corn until tender, drain; cool. Combine corn, green pepper, onion and parsley. In small bowl, combine mayonnaise and sour cream. Dissolve bouillon in vinegar; stir into mayonnaise mixture with salt and pepper. Toss with corn to coat. Cover, chill thoroughly. Cook bacon crisp; drain and crumble. Add bacon to corn mixture and toss. Serve on lettuce.

Green and Orange Salad   Serves 4

1 16-oz. can peas, drained
½ cup shredded Cheddar
    cheese
2 T. chopped pimento
⅓ cup Italian dressing
    dash onion powder
    lettuce

Combine peas, cheese and pimento. Mix salad dressing and onion powder; toss lightly with pea mixture. Chill. Serve on lettuce-lined plates.

Filled Melon Fruit Salad   Serves 10 to 12

1 honeydew melon or
   cantaloupe, halved
   and seeded
1 T. unflavored gelatin
¼ cup warm water
6 oz. cream cheese,
   softened
2 T. condensed milk
½ T. lemon juice
2 cups fruit

Soften gelatin in water. Beat in cream cheese, milk and lemon juice. Fold in fruit (such as strawberries, diced peaches, seedless grapes, blueberries, pitted cherries etc.) and pour into melon cavity. Chill until set. When ready to serve, carefully slice into wedges.

Note: Unusual and pretty.

Gazpacho Jiggler   Yields 6 cups

2 cups chopped tomatoes
½ cup chopped green chile
½ cup chopped celery
½ cup chopped onion
2 T. chopped parsley
1½ tsp. salt
¼ tsp. pepper
2 T. tarragon vinegar
   dash of Worcestershire
   sauce
1 6-oz. package lemon
   gelatin
2 cups boiling water
1½ cups cold water

Combine vegetables, seasonings, vinegar and Worcestershire sauce in bowl. Dissolve gelatin in boiling water. Add cold water. Chill until starting to set. Stir in vegetable mixture. Chill.

Note: Jiggler may be made a day ahead. This is a very attractive salad presented on lettuce leaves.

Fresh Southwest Salad

Serves 6 to 8

2   cups broccoli florets
2   cups cauliflower florets
1   8-oz. can pitted ripe
      olives, drained
¼   lb. salami, julienned
¼   lb. cheese, cubed
1   8-oz. bottle Italian
      dressing

Combine vegetables, salami and cheese. Pour dressing over all, mix well and serve.

Note: Use your imagination on this salad. Almost any variety of vegetables may be used. It is a colorful salad that can be prepared as much as a day ahead and is a nice addition to a party table.

Seasoned Salad

Serves 12

2   avocados, peeled, pitted
      and diced
½   lb. mushrooms, cleaned
      and sliced
½   head cauliflower,
      separated into florets
2   cups Italian dressing

Combine vegetables. Pour dressing over vegetables, mix to coat and marinate at least 1 hour, or overnight.

Green, Red and Bleu Salad

Serves 10

2   10-oz. packages frozen
      cut green beans
1   medium red onion,
      sliced
1   2.2-oz. can sliced black
      olives, drained
2   oz. bleu cheese,
      crumbled
½   cup prepared Italian
      dressing

Bring 1 quart water to boil. Add beans and cook until just tender, about 2 minutes. Drain well. Transfer to large bowl. Mix in onion, olives and cheese. Stir in dressing and toss thoroughly.

Golden Chicken Rice Salad   Serves 4

1 12-oz. package frozen
   rice pilaf
¼ cup mayonnaise
¼ cup chopped green
   pepper
2 T. sliced green onion
½ tsp. dried, crushed
   tarragon
2 cups cooked cubed
   chicken
4 fresh peaches, peeled,
   pitted and sliced
   lettuce

Prepare rice pilaf according to package directions; cool in mixing bowl. Stir in mayonnaise, green pepper, onion and tarragon. Add chicken; toss lightly to coat. Cover and chill. Shortly before serving, add peaches and toss. Serve in lettuce cups or on lettuce leaves.

Mexican Salad   Serves 8

1 6-oz. can pitted, ripe
   olives, sliced
1 head lettuce, chopped
1 16-oz. can pinto beans,
   drained
2 tomatoes, chopped
2 T. diced green chile
1 avocado, mashed
½ cup sour cream
2 T. Italian dressing
1 T. minced onion
¾ tsp. chili powder
½ tsp. salt
⅛ tsp. pepper
½ cup grated Cheddar
   cheese
½ cup crushed tortilla
   chips

Combine olives, lettuce, beans, tomatoes, and chile; chill. Blend avocado, sour cream, dressing, onion and seasonings. Pour over lettuce mixture and toss to coat. Top with cheese and chips.

Herring Salad

Serves 8

1 lb. herring, either in
    cream or wine
4 apples, peeled and diced
2 eggs, hard boiled
1 lb. cooked potatoes,
    peeled and diced
1 13-oz. can diced beets,
    drained, liquid
    reserved
2 pickle spears, diced
3 T. mayonnaise
2 T. sour cream

Cut herring pieces in half. Add pickles, eggs, potatoes and apples. Then add beets, mayonnaise, sour cream and ⅓ cup beet juice. Mix all together until pink and store overnight in refrigerator. Serve on lettuce leaves.

Instant Fruit Salad

Serves 10

4 cups fruit (fresh, frozen
    or canned), diced
1 cup sour cream
½ cup miniature
    marshmallows
½ cup nuts, chopped
    maraschino cherries

Drain fruit. Add sour cream, nuts and marshmallows. Mix well. Garnish with cherries. Serve or refrigerate.
Note: What a great, quick salad. So pretty with various colored fruits.

Lemon Mushroom Salad

Serves 4

1 lb. mushrooms
½ cup olive oil
3 T. lemon juice
1 T. Dijon mustard
½ tsp. salt
¼ tsp. pepper
    lettuce leaves

Slice mushrooms. In screw-top jar combine oil, lemon juice, mustard, salt and pepper. Cover and shake well. Pour mixture over mushrooms; toss to coat. Let stand at room temperature for 1 hour, stirring occasionally. Serve mushrooms on lettuce leaves.

Pinon Salad

Serves 2

¼ cup pinon nuts
1 small head of butter lettuce, torn into bite-size pieces
2 oranges, peeled
3 T. vegetable oil
3 T. fresh orange juice
½ tsp. fresh lemon juice dash of cinnamon

Preheat oven to 350°. Toast pinon nuts 5 minutes, until golden; cool. Section or slice oranges. Cover and refrigerate. Combine oil, orange juice, lemon juice and cinnamon in a jar, shake well and refrigerate. When ready to serve, toss lettuce, oranges and nuts. Shake dressing, pour on salad, toss and serve. *Note: Recipe may be doubled or tripled.*

Salad Souffle

Serves 10 to 12

1 8-oz. can crushed pineapple, drained, and liquid reserved
1 3-oz. package orange-flavored gelatin
¾ cup boiling water
¾ cup mayonnaise
1 cup finely shredded cabbage
1 cup shredded carrot
½ cup raisins
½ cup chopped walnuts
3 egg whites, stiffly beaten

Dissolve gelatin in boiling water. Add reserved pineapple liquid. Beat in mayonnaise. Freeze mixture in loaf pan until firm 1 inch from edge, but soft in center, about 20 minutes. Put in large bowl and beat until fluffy. Fold in pineapple, cabbage, carrot, raisins and walnuts, then egg whites. Pour into 2 quart souffle dish. Chill until set. *Note: An elegant side dish that's simple to make.*

Broccoli Salad   Serves 8

1 lb. frozen chopped
      broccoli, thawed
8 slices bacon, cooked
      and crumbled
½ cup raisins
1 cup chopped walnuts
½ cup chopped onions
¾ cup mayonnaise
2 T. sugar
2 T. vinegar

Combine broccoli, bacon, raisins, nuts and onions. Mix mayonnaise, sugar and vinegar; pour over vegetable mixture. Refrigerate.

Note: Make this pretty salad early in the day, allowing flavors to blend and avoiding last minute rush.

Sour Cream and Cucumbers   Serves 4

2 medium cucumbers,
      thinly sliced
½ tsp. salt
1 T. sugar
¼ tsp. dill weed
      dash pepper
½ cup sour cream
1 T. vinegar

In medium bowl, sprinkle salt over cucumbers. Let stand 20 minutes; drain. Add remaining ingredients; toss lightly. Cover and chill until ready to serve.

Strawberry Salad   Serves 8

1 3-oz. package
      strawberry gelatin
1 cup boiling water
1 10-oz. package frozen
      sliced strawberries,
      partially thawed
1 cup sliced bananas,
      cubed or mashed
1 10½-oz. can crushed
      pineapple, drained
1 pint sour cream

Dissolve gelatin in boiling water; cool. Add strawberries, bananas and pineapple. Pour half of the mixture into a shallow dish. Chill until partially set. Spread sour cream mixture on top of the gelatin. Layer remaining gelatin mixture over sour cream and chill until firm.

Super Simple Salad

Serves 4

½ medium head lettuce
1 avocado, diced
3 green onions, diced
¼ cup sunflower seeds
 shelled
2 oz. bleu cheese,
 crumbled
¼ cup sweetened rice
 vinegar

Chop lettuce. Combine with avocado, onions, sunflower seeds and bleu cheese. Sprinkle with vinegar. Toss and serve.

Note: Recipe can be doubled or tripled.

Super Caesar Salad

Serves 8

⅓ cup olive oil
1 clove garlic, minced
2 raw eggs
4 anchovy fillets
2 T. lemon juice
4 T. wine vinegar
 dash Worcestershire
 sauce
½ cup Parmesan cheese
¼ cup bleu cheese,
 crumbled
½ cup croutons
3 quarts Romaine lettuce

In large salad bowl, combine olive oil, garlic, eggs and anchovies. Mix well. Add lemon juice, vinegar and Worcestershire sauce, then cheeses. Add ½ cup croutons, then lettuce. Toss well and serve immediately, with additional croutons, if desired.

Tricolor Salad

Serves 2

 lettuce for two
4 oz. mushrooms, sliced
10 cherry tomatoes, halved
1 tsp. Dijon mustard
1½ tsp. red wine vinegar
2 T. olive oil
 salt and pepper to taste

Combine lettuce, mushrooms and tomatoes. Mix mustard and vinegar, gradually whisk in oil. Season with salt and pepper. Pour over salad and toss.

Note: Recipe can be doubled.

Tomato Refresher   Serves 8

2 bell peppers, diced
⅔ cup celery, diced
1 onion, diced
1 T. salt
¼ tsp. pepper
¼ cup balsamic vinegar
¼ cup sugar
1 cup cold water
6 medium tomatoes,
     sliced

Combine first eight ingredients. Pour over tomatoes. Cover and chill 4 hours. Serve chilled.
Note: This makes mid-winter tomatoes taste garden fresh.

Sweet and Savory Salad   Serves 8

1 head lettuce, torn
2 avocados, peeled and
     diced
1 apple, cut into chunks
1 8-oz. can mandarin
     orange slices,
     drained
½ purple onion, sliced
⅓ cup raisins
⅓ cup slivered almonds
¼ cup vinegar
½ cup olive oil
1 clove garlic, minced
1 T. Dijon mustard
   salt and pepper to taste

Combine lettuce, avocados, apple, orange slices, onion, raisins and almonds. Whisk vinegar, oil, garlic, mustard, salt and pepper and pour over salad. Toss and serve.
Note: This delicious salad can be made early in the day with the apple and avocados in the bottom of the salad bowl, topped with the oranges, lettuce, etc., cover and refrigerate. Dress and toss salad when ready to serve. This is a guaranteed hit.

Lettuce with Hot Dressing   Serves 6

1	large head of lettuce
1	cup sliced green onions
12	slices bacon
½	cup vinegar
½	cup water
8	tsp. sugar
1	tsp. salt

Tear lettuce and mix with green onions. Cook bacon until crisp; drain and crumble. Combine bacon fat, vinegar, water, sugar, salt and bacon; cook and stir until boiling. Pour hot dressing over lettuce; serve salad immediately.

Vegetable Marinade   Serves 8

2½	cups salad oil
1	cup white vinegar
1	bunch chives, chopped
1	bunch green onions, chopped
2½	T. sugar
1½	T. salt
1	T. lemon juice
1	T. minced garlic
2	tsp. Worcestershire sauce
2	tsp. bottled browning sauce
⅛	tsp. prepared mustard
1	lb. fresh mushrooms, cleaned

Whisk all ingredients except mushrooms in blender until well combined. Pour over mushrooms. Cover and marinate in refrigerator overnight.

Note: This marinade also works well with sliced zucchini, cauliflower or broccoli. Vegetables will keep well in marinade several days in the refrigerator.

Garbanzo and Vegetable Salad   Serves 12

2 15-oz. cans garbanzo
    beans, drained and
    rinsed
2 medium tomatoes,
    chopped
3 green onions, thinly
    sliced
3 radishes, thinly sliced
8 mushrooms, thinly
    sliced
¾ cup snipped fresh
    parsley
¾ cup grated cheddar
    cheese
½ cup lemon juice
⅓ cup olive oil
½ tsp. ground cumin
½ tsp. salt
¼ tsp. black pepper

Combine beans, tomatoes, onions, radishes, mushrooms, parsley and cheese. Mix remaining ingredients and pour over bean mixture. Cover and refrigerate at least 1 hour.

Note: Keeps refrigerated up to one week.

El Adobe Fruit Salad   Serves 8

4 T. frozen lemonade
    concentrate, thawed
4 T. salad oil
4 T. honey
2 tsp. poppy seed
2 cups pineapple chunks
2 cups strawberries,
    quartered
2 kiwi, sliced
2 bananas, sliced

In blender combine lemonade, oil, honey and poppy seed. Blend 10 seconds. Combine fruit in bowl and top with dressing.

Heavenly Hash Salad   Serves 12

2 T. cornstarch
½ cup plus 2 T. sugar
1 cup pineapple syrup
   and water
2 eggs, separated
1 20-oz. can pineapple
   tidbits, drained and
   reserved
¼ cup chopped walnuts
3 cups miniature
   marshmallows
6 bananas, sliced
   lettuce

Combine cornstarch, ½ cup sugar, syrup and egg yolks in saucepan. Mix well and cook 5 minutes until thickened. Cool. Whip egg whites until stiff peaks form. Add 2 T. sugar and whip again until stiff peaks form. Fold whites into yolk mixture. Add pineapple, nuts, marshmallows and bananas. Chill. Serve on lettuce.

North German Salad   Serves 4

¼ lb. boiled or baked ham,
   minced
2 apples, peeled, cored
   and diced
2 4-oz. cans tiny shrimp,
   drained
1 tsp. prepared mustard
2 T. salad dressing
1 T. sour cream
¼ tsp. paprika
½ tsp. garlic salt
¼ tsp. ground cumin
¼ tsp. ground ginger
   lettuce

Combine all ingredients. Chill. Serve on lettuce leaves. Garnish with medium shrimp and parsley if desired.

Green Bean Salad   Serves 4

3 cups torn lettuce
1 15½-oz. can French-cut
   green beans, drained
   and chilled
3 T. grated Parmesan
   cheese
⅓ cup Italian dressing

Combine lettuce, green beans and Parmesan. Toss with dressing to coat.

Potato Salad Dressing   Yields 1½ cups

2 eggs, beaten
½ cup sugar
1 T. flour
¾ cup cream
¼ cup vinegar
1 tsp. prepared yellow
   mustard

Combine all ingredients in saucepan and cook, stirring until thickened. Remove from heat, cool, cover and refrigerate until needed. Keeps several weeks.

Seasoned Macaroni Salad   Serves 4

2½ cups cooked macaroni
1   tsp. salt
1   tsp. oil
½   cup peas, cooked and
    drained
2   T. minced onion
1   cup cottage cheese
½   cup mayonnaise
½   cup diced carrots,
    cooked
¼   cup diced green chile

Combine all ingredients and mix thoroughly to coat macaroni. Refrigerate until serving.

Bacon and Chicken Sandwich Filling

Yields 1½ cups

8 slices bacon, cooked and crumbled
1 cup chicken, cooked and chopped
¼ cup mayonnaise
1 T. chopped pimento
¼ tsp. salt
   dash of pepper

Combine all ingredients. Refrigerate.
Note: Delicious!

Cheese and Nut Sandwich Filling

Yields 2 cups

1 3-ounce package cream cheese, softened
1 cup chopped pecans
¾ cup drained crushed pineapple

Combine all ingredients. Refrigerate.
Note: This is good in sandwiches or on crackers for a snack.

Cornish Pasties (Paasties!)   Serves 6

6 Pepperidge Farm puff pastry patty shells, thawed
1 15-oz. can roast beef or corned beef hash
⅓ cup chopped onion
⅓ cup chopped carrot
½ tsp. Worcestershire sauce

Preheat oven to 400°. On floured surface, roll each patty shell to a 6-inch circle. Combine hash, onion, carrot and Worcestershire Sauce. Place ⅓ cup of mixture on half of each circle. Fold over and seal edges with fork. Brush with beaten egg or milk, if desired. Place on baking pan. Bake for 35 minutes or until brown. Serve with warmed ketchup, if desired.

Patio Hoagie

Serves 8

1½ lb. ground beef
1 8-oz. can tomato sauce
8 slices American cheese
¼ cup chopped green
    onions
2 tsp. beef bouillon
½ tsp. garlic powder
1 1-lb. loaf French bread
1 tomato, sliced
1 green pepper, cut into
    rings

Preheat oven to 400°. In skillet brown meat. Pour off fat. Stir in tomato sauce, 3 slices of American cheese, onions, bouillon and garlic. Cover. Simmer 10 minutes or until bouillon dissolves. Stir occasionally. Slice off top of bread and scoop out center. Place loaf on large sheet of foil for wrapping. Spoon meat mixture into loaf. Cut remaining cheese slices in half diagonally, layer alternately with tomato and pepper on meat. Replace bread top. Tightly wrap in foil. Bake 20 minutes or until hot. Slice and serve.

Shrimp Sandwich Filling

Yields 2 cups

1 egg, hardboiled
1⅓ cups chopped shrimp
¼ cup chopped celery
2 T. lemon juice
¼ tsp. salt
    dash pepper
¼ cup mayonnaise

Combine all ingredients. Refrigerate.
Note: Very good!

Southwest Bar-B-Qued Beef   Serves 20 to 24

4 - 5 lb. beef roast
1 10-oz. can beef bouillon soup
1 10-oz. can water
1 envelope dry onion soup mix
   Bull's-Eye Bar-B-Q Sauce

Cook beef, bouillon, water and onion soup in crock pot for 10 hours. Cool in broth. String beef with two forks. Combine 2 cups of broth, beef and as much bar-b-que sauce as required for size of roast.

Note: Freezes well. Great to have on hand for a big group. Heat in pan or microwave and serve on buns. Other uses for broth: Skim fat from remaining broth. Place hamburgers in deep pan, top with above gravy and bake until done. Mushrooms are a nice addition to this. Broth is also good added to sauces or soups.

Open English Muffins   Serves 4

2 English muffins, split and toasted
2 T. butter or margarine, soft
4 tomato slices
8 slices bacon, cooked
8 slices Swiss cheese

Place muffin halves on microwave safe plate. Spread evenly with butter. Top each with tomato, 2 slices of bacon and with cheese. Microwave on high for 1 minute or until cheese melts.

Brunchwich   **Serves 6**

1   **loaf French bread**
½   **lb. ham, sliced**
½   **lb. mozzarella cheese,
      sliced**
¼   **cup milk**
2   **eggs**
¼   **cup butter or margarine**
1   **cup maple syrup**

Cut 12 slices of bread, each ½-inch thick. Fit ham and cheese on 6 slices; top with remaining slices. Beat milk and eggs. Dip sandwiches into egg mixture until well coated on both sides. In skillet heat butter and cook sandwiches 15 minutes until golden on both sides. In microwave heat syrup 1 minute on high until hot, but not boiling. Serve hot sandwiches with hot syrup alongside.
Note: Nice for ladies' brunch.

Cheese Muffins   **Serves 48**

2   **cups grated Cheddar
      cheese**
½   **cup mayonnaise**
¼   **cup thinly sliced green
      onions**
2   **T. chopped pitted green
      olives, well drained**
1   **tsp. capers, well drained**
6   **English muffins, halved**
1   **T. Parmesan cheese**

Preheat oven to 350°. Combine Cheddar cheese, mayonnaise, onions, olives, and capers. Spread on muffins. Top with Parmesan. Cut muffin-halves into quarters. Place on ungreased cookie sheet. Bake 15 minutes or until cheese bubbles.
Note: Refrigerate up to 24 hours or freeze.

Breads, Pancakes, and Coffee Cakes

HOLLY HOCKS ROAD

Manzano, New Mexico, a tiny village nestled in the mountain range for which it was named, lies Southeast of Albuquerque. The name means *Apple Tree*, which tradition claims were in two old orchards planted during the mission period, before 1676. They are said to be the oldest apple orchards in America. Whatever the season, the area is always beautiful.

Apple Cranberry Bread

Yields 1 loaf

2 cups flour
1 tsp. baking soda
1 tsp. cardamon
½ tsp. salt
½ cup butter
1 cup sugar
2 eggs
1 tsp. vanilla
½ tsp. almond extract
⅓ cup orange juice
1 cup chopped apples
½ cup walnuts
½ cup chopped
    cranberries

Preheat oven to 350°. Grease loaf pan. Mix flour, soda, cardamon and salt. Beat butter and sugar. Add eggs, one at a time, beat in extracts. Add flour mixture, alternately with orange juice in 3 batches, beating just until blended. Stir in apples and cranberries. Pour into pan. Bake 50 minutes, or until pick inserted near center comes out clean. Cool 10 minutes, remove from pan. *Note: Freezes well. It is especially pretty for Christmas!*

Bishop's Bread

Yields 1 loaf

1 cup sugar
3 eggs
1½ cups flour
1½ tsp. baking powder
1 cup whole walnuts
1 cups whole brazil nuts
1 cup whole maraschino
    cherries, drained
1 cup whole pitted dates
1 8-oz. bar semi-sweet
    chocolate, cut in ½-
    inch chunks

Preheat oven to 325°. Beat sugar and eggs, then flour and baking powder. Mix (by hand or cherries will crush) in nuts, cherries, dates and chocolate. Line 9-inch loaf pan with waxed paper. Pour batter into pan, covering batter with excess paper. Bake for 1 hour and 25 minutes. Uncover for last 30 minutes of baking. *Note: Freezes well. This is a Norwegian Christmas "MUST."*

Best Broccoli Corn Bread   Serves 24 to 30

¾ cup margarine
2 8½-oz. boxes Jiffy Corn
   Bread mix
4 eggs, beaten
1 8-oz. carton cottage
   cheese
1 8-oz. package frozen
   chopped broccoli,
   thawed
1 small onion, chopped

Preheat oven to 350°. Melt margarine in 9 x 13-inch pan. Mix rest of ingredients in pan. Bake for 45 minutes. Cut and serve warm.

Note: Freezes well. May be made in greased muffin cups, which reduces baking time to about 20 minutes.

Healthy Bread   Yields 2 loaves

2 cups All-Bran
3 cups hot water
3 cups white flour, ap-
   proximately
1 cup whole wheat flour
1 cup oatmeal
½ cup dry skim milk
2 T. dry yeast
½ cup honey
⅓ cup oil
4 egg whites
1 cup raisins (optional)

Pour hot water over All-Bran and set aside. Mix flours, oatmeal, skim milk powder, and yeast in large bowl. Add remaining ingredients and additional flour, if required, to knead until smooth. Place in greased container, cover and let rise 1 hour until double in size. Knead dough until all air bubbles are out. Divide in half. Shape into two loaves and place in greased loaf pans, cover. Let rise again, about 30 minutes or until almost double in size. Uncover and place in preheated 350° oven for 35 minutes or until golden and cooked through.

Note: Freezes well. Tasty and good for you. Try it toasted with homemade jam!

Easter Bread

Yields 1 tube pan loaf

- 5 cups flour, approximately
- 1 cup sugar
- 1 T. yeast
- 1 tsp. salt
- ½ cup warm milk
- ¼ cup warm water
- ½ cup butter or margarine, melted
- 5 eggs, room temperature
- 1 T. anise extract

Combine dry ingredients in bowl. Make a well in center and add milk, water, butter, eggs and anise. Knead. Add flour as required. Let rise in greased, covered bowl until double in size. Knead and shape, cover and let rise again. Bake at 350° for 45 minutes, or until golden and baked through.

Note: Two cups of whole wheat flour may be substituted for all white flour. After second rising you may insert colored boiled eggs near top of bread. It gives an aura of Easter.

Pineapple-Zucchini Bread

Yields 2 loaves

- 3 eggs, beaten
- 1 cup oil
- 2 cups sugar
- 1½ tsp. vanilla
- 2 cups grated zucchini
- 1 cup crushed pineapple, drained
- 3 cups flour
- 1 tsp. baking soda
- 1 tsp. baking powder
- 1 tsp. salt

Preheat oven to 350°. Grease 2 regular loaf pans or 5 mini loaf pans. Beat eggs, oil, sugar and vanilla. Add the zucchini, pineapple, flour, baking soda, baking powder and salt. Beat well. Pour batter into pans. Bake for 45 minutes or until tester comes out clean when inserted near center of loaf.

Note: Freezes well.

Corn Bread Delight

Yields 1 loaf

2 eggs, beaten
1 8-oz. package cream
   cheese, softened
1 cup cream corn
1 cup cornmeal
1½ tsp. baking powder
⅔ cup oil
1 4-oz. can chopped green
   chile
1 cup grated Cheddar
   cheese

Preheat oven to 325°. Grease loaf pan or 8 x 8-inch pan. Mix ingredients in order given. Blend well and bake for 45 minutes or until done. *Note: So simple, so tasty! Freezes well.*

Poppy Seed Bread

Yields 2 loaves

BREAD:
3 cups flour
1 tsp. salt
1½ tsp. baking powder
3 eggs, beaten
2¼ cups sugar
1½ tsp. vanilla
1 T. poppy seeds
1⅛ cups oil
1½ tsp. almond extract
1½ tsp. butter flavoring
1½ cups milk
GLAZE:
¾ cup powdered sugar
¼ cup orange juice
½ tsp. vanilla
½ tsp. almond extract
½ tsp. butter flavoring

Preheat oven to 350°. Grease 2 loaf pans. Mix ingredients and pour into pans. Bake for 60 minutes. Cool. Combine all glaze ingredients and pour over bread. *Note: Freezes well.*

Creamed Corn Biscuits

Serves 12

2 cups biscuit mix
1 15-oz. can cream corn
½ cup butter, melted
   flour

Preheat oven to 450°. Mix biscuit mix and corn. Roll out dough on floured board. Cut out biscuits. Pour butter in baking pan. Dip top and bottom of biscuits in butter. Bake in pan for 10 minutes or until golden.

Note: Simple to make. You can't eat just one!

Italiano Dinner Rolls

Yields 16 rolls

4-5 cups flour
2 packages dry yeast
1½ tsp. Italian seasoning
1 cup milk
½ cup water
2 T. sugar
4 T. butter or margarine
1 tsp. garlic salt
2 eggs
¾ cup grated Parmesan cheese, divided

Combine 1½ cups flour, yeast and Italian seasoning. Heat milk, water, sugar, 2 T. butter and salt until warm (115 to 120°); add to flour mixture. Add eggs and beat at low speed of mixer for ½ minute. Beat 3 minutes at high speed. Stir in ½ cup Parmesan cheese. Add flour as needed for stiff dough. Knead on floured board. Place in greased bowl. Cover; let rise 45 minutes in warm place until double in bulk. Punch down, let rest 10 minutes. Shape into 16 balls. Dip tops into 2 T. melted butter, then into ¼ cup Parmesan. Place rolls in 2 greased 9-inch round baking pans. Cover; let rise 15 minutes until nearly double. Bake at 375° for 20 minutes.

Parmesan Puffs   **Serves 10**

1 11-oz. package
   refrigerator biscuits
¼ cup butter, melted
⅓ cup grated Parmesan
   cheese

Preheat oven to 475°. Dip biscuit tops into butter, then cheese. Place biscuits cheese-side up on baking sheet. Bake 8 minutes until golden.
Note: So simple you must try them. Freezes well. Reheat in microwave.

Super Healthy Muffins   **Yields 8 dozen muffins**

4 cups All-Bran buds or
   40% Bran cereal
2 cups boiling water
1 cup butter or margarine
3 cups sugar
4 eggs, beaten
4 cups buttermilk
5 cups flour
1 cup oatmeal
5 tsp. baking soda
2 cups 100% bran cereal
2 cups raisins
1 cup chopped dates

Pour water over bran buds, let stand one hour. Cream butter and sugar, add eggs. Stir flour and soda together. Add flour, fruit and buttermilk alternately to butter mixture. Add 100% bran and soaked buds. Bake immediately or refrigerate. To bake, heat oven to 400°. Grease muffin tins, fill ¾ full and bake for 25 minutes.
Note: These taste good and are good for you! Even children like them. The batter can be held in the refrigerator for several weeks and baked as required (1 pint of batter makes 12 muffins) or bake the entire batch, freeze and simply microwave/defrost as needed.

Seasoned Sticks

Yields 2 dozen

1 sheet Pepperidge Farm puff pastry
⅛ cup milk
1 tsp. Italian seasoning
¼ cup Parmesan cheese
½ tsp. garlic salt
¼ tsp. paprika

Preheat oven to 375°. On lightly floured board, roll puff pastry to ⅛ inch thickness. Place on cookie sheet. Moisten top with milk, then sprinkle with Italian seasoning, Parmesan, garlic salt and paprika. With a sharp knife, cut pastry in thirds, then make ½ inch cuts in the opposite direction, to form sticks. Bake 15 to 20 minutes or until golden.

Strawberry Bread

Yields 2 loaves

3 cups flour
½ tsp. cinnamon
1 tsp. baking soda
1 tsp. salt
5 eggs, beaten
1½ cups cooking oil
2 10-oz. boxes diced frozen strawberries, thawed
1¼ cups chopped pecans

Preheat oven to 325°. Mix flour, cinnamon, baking soda, and salt. Beat eggs, oil, strawberries, sugar, pecans, and flour mixture. Divide between 2 8 x 5-inch loaf pans. Bake for one hour.
Note: Serve with cream cheese.

Moist Sour Bread

Yields 2 loaves

5 cups self-rising flour
5 T. sugar
1½ cups sour cream
1 12-oz. can beer

Preheat oven to 325°. Combine flour and sugar. Add sour cream and beer; mix well. Pour into 2 loaf pans and bake one hour, or until done.

Sunday Morning Pancakes   Serves 1

1 T. butter
1 egg
¼ cup milk
¼ cup flour
   dash salt

Preheat oven to 425°. Place butter in 8 inch pie pan and melt. In blender beat egg, milk, flour and salt. Pour into pie pan and bake for 10 minutes or until puffed and starting to brown. Serve with lemon juice and powdered sugar, or fruit.

Note: Recipe may be doubled, tripled, etc. as long as enough pie pans are available.

Upside-Down Blueberry Pancakes
Serves 4 to 6

1 cup pancake mix
2 T. butter or margarine
1 16-oz. can blueberries

Preheat oven to 350°. Prepare pancake mix according to package directions. Set aside. In 10-inch pie plate melt butter and remove from heat. Drain blueberries. Spoon berries in bottom of pan, carefully pour batter atop. Bake 18 minutes. Loosen edges of pancake and invert onto serving plate. Cut in wedges and serve with syrup.

Note: This simple breakfast can be made with almost any fruit, fresh, frozen or canned. Just be sure to drain well. Kids love it. Freezes well.

SOUTHWEST SEASONS SOUTHWEST SEASONS SOUTHWEST SEASONS SOUTHWEST SEASONS SOUTHWEST

Polish Pancakes   Serves 12

4 T. butter, softened
1½ cups sugar
1 egg
1 cup milk
2 cups flour
3 tsp. baking powder
1½ T. sugar
½ tsp. cinnamon

Preheat oven to 350°. Grease a 13 x 9 x 2-inch baking pan. Combine 3 T. butter and sugar. Add egg, milk, flour, and baking powder. Mix until smooth. Pour into pan and bake for 30 minutes. Top with 1 T. butter, cinnamon and sugar.

Refrigerator Pancakes   Yields 1 gallon

2 T. baking soda
2 T. sugar
1 tsp. salt
1 quart buttermilk
2 T. baking powder
4 cups flour
6 eggs, beaten
¼ cup vegetable oil
1 package yeast
1 cup cream

Add soda, sugar and salt to buttermilk. Stir baking powder into flour, add to buttermilk mixture, then mix in remaining ingredients. Store refrigerated in gallon container. Keeps up to 2 weeks.

Company French Toast   Serves 8

1 loaf French bread
8 large eggs
3 cups milk
4 tsp. sugar
1 T. vanilla
2 T. butter

Grease 9 x 13-inch pan. Cut bread into 1-inch thick slices; arrange in single layer in pan. Mix remaining ingredients in blender; pour over bread. Cover and refrigerate 4 to 36 hours. Uncover and bake for 45 minutes at 350° until bread is puffy and golden. Let stand 5 minutes before serving.

Cherry Puff
Serves 8

1 17¼-oz. package
    Pepperidge Farm
    Puff Pastry Sheets
1 8-oz. package cream
    cheese
1 22-oz. can cherry pie
    filling
2 cups powdered sugar
4 T. milk

Preheat oven to 350°. Roll each sheet of puff pastry out to 14 x 11 inches. Slice cream cheese into thin slices and arrange down center ⅓ of both pastries. Pour filling over cheese. Cut outer edges of pastry into one inch strips and braid over filling. Bake about 20 to 30 minutes until puffy and golden. Combine sugar and milk; frost puffs. *Note: Freezes well. With ready made pastry and filling, this is made in minutes. It can be served as a coffee cake or as a dessert.*

Cinnamon Coffee Cake
Serves 8 to 10

1½ cups flour
1½ tsp. baking powder
1 cup sour cream
1 tsp. baking soda
½ cup butter, softened
1⅓ cups sugar
2 large eggs
1 tsp. vanilla
⅓ cup brown sugar
1 T. cinnamon

Preheat oven to 350°. Butter 10 x 10 x 2-inch baking dish. In bowl mix flour and baking powder. In another bowl stir together sour cream and baking soda. In mixer cream butter and 1 cup sugar; add eggs and vanilla. Mix well. Pour coffee cake into pan. (Leavening causes batter to rise; will overflow, if pan is too small.) Combine brown sugar and ⅓ cup sugar with cinnamon. Swirl mixture into coffee cake with knife. Bake 45 minutes.

R and S Coffee Cake   Serves 15

3½ cups flour, divided
2¾ cups sugar, divided
1 tsp. baking soda
1 tsp. baking powder
1¼ cups butter or
    margarine
1 cup buttermilk
2 eggs, beaten
1 tsp. vanilla
3 cups fresh rhubarb, cut
    in 1-inch pieces
1 16-oz. package frozen
    sliced strawberries,
    thawed
2 T. lemon juice
⅓ cup cornstarch

Preheat oven to 350°. Grease 13 x 9-inch baking pan. In mixing bowl stir 3 cups flour, 1 cup sugar, soda, and baking powder. Cut in 1 cup butter to fine crumbs. Beat together buttermilk, eggs and vanilla; add to dry ingredients. Stir to moisten. Spread half the batter in baking pan. In saucepan combine rhubarb and strawberries. Cook fruit 5 minutes, covered. Add 2 T. lemon juice. Combine 1 cup sugar and ⅓ cup cornstarch; add to rhubarb mixture. Cook and stir 5 minutes until thickened and bubbly. Cool. Spread rhubarb filling over batter. Spoon remaining batter in small mounds atop filling. Combine remaining ¾ cup sugar and ½ cup flour; cut in ¼ cup butter to fine crumbs. Sprinkle over batter in pan. Bake for 45 minutes.

Effortless Apple Tart   Serves 6

1 sheet Pepperidge Farm
    puff pastry
2 cups apples slices
2 T. butter, melted
2 T. sugar
⅓ cup apricot preserves,
    melted

Preheat oven to 400°. Pat pastry smoothly in 9½-inch tart pan and pierce with fork. Arrange apples on pastry. Sprinkle with butter, then sugar. Bake for 35 minutes or until done. Top with preserves.

Coffee Cake with Espresso   Serves 10 to 12

1½   cups butter
2   cups sugar
4   large eggs
4   tsp. vanilla
1   tsp. baking powder
¼   tsp. baking soda
4   cups flour
2   cups sour cream
8   T. instant espresso
6   T. hot water

Preheat oven to 350°. Grease and flour 2½ quart Bundt pan. With mixer, cream butter and sugar until light and fluffy. Add eggs, beating after each. Beat in vanilla, baking powder and soda. Mix well. Add flour alternately with sour cream, blending well. Dissolve 4 T. espresso in 2 T. hot water. Transfer ⅓ of batter to another bowl and stir in espresso mixture (batter will be loose). Spoon half of remaining plain batter into pan, spread evenly. Top with coffee batter. Then top with remaining plain batter and spread evenly. Bake for 1 hour or until tester comes out clean. Let cool in pan for 30 minutes before inverting to cool completely. Combine 1½ cups powdered sugar with 4 T. espresso dissolved in 4 T. hot water. Pour coffee into sugar and mix. Spread on cake and serve.

Note: May be frozen before frosting. Dense, moist, chewy and delicious!

Entrees

SUMMER'S BOUNTY

Velarde, New Mexico stands in the center of lush vegetable gardens and fruit orchards. The countryside is wonderful in late summer and autumn when vegetable and fruit stands appear along the roads offering an astonishing variety of home grown produce. This tiny business never fails to stop traffic on the journey to Taos.

Beef Bourguignonne

Serves 5

1 T. butter or margarine
1½ lb. sirloin steak, cut
  into 1-inch cubes
1½ cups fresh mushrooms,
  sliced
1 medium onion, sliced
1 clove garlic, minced
⅛ tsp. pepper
1 green pepper, cut into
  1-inch pieces
1 1¼-oz. package beef-
  mushroom soup mix
1 cup water
½ cup Burgundy wine
1 16-oz. can onions,
  drained

In large skillet, brown meat in butter. Add mushrooms, onion and garlic; cook until tender. Add remaining ingredients; simmer covered, 20 minutes or until meat is tender, stirring occasionally.

Brief Beef and Broccoli

Serves 4

2 T. oyster sauce
2 T. Chinese rice wine
1 T. soy sauce
1 tsp. cornstarch
1 lb. fresh broccoli,
  trimmed and peeled
1 T. oil
2 garlic cloves, minced
½ lb. lean beef, thinly
  sliced
½ cup frozen pearl onions,
  thawed and drained
¼ cup diced pimento,
  drained

In small bowl combine oyster sauce, rice wine, soy sauce and cornstarch. Mix well; set aside. Boil broccoli in water 10 minutes until crisp-tender. Drain. Cut off florets, slice stems diagonally. Heat wok or skillet. Add oil and swirl to coat. Add half of garlic and stir-fry briefly. Blend in beef and broccoli stems and stir-fry 2 minutes. Add florets, onions, pimento, remaining garlic, and sauce from bowl. Cover and cook 2 minutes until vegetables are crisp-tender. Serve over noodles or rice.

Beef Brisket

Serves 8 to 10

4 to 5 lb. brisket
½ cup brown sugar
½ cup vinegar
¼ cup ketchup
4 dashes Worcestershire
   sauce
2 T. soy sauce

Preheat oven to 350°. Combine all ingredients except meat. Cover meat and bake for 2 hours. Reduce heat to 300° and add ⅓ of sauce. Bake 2 more hours, adding sauce hourly.
Note: Add ½ cup chopped green chile for Southwestern flair. Freezes well.

Beef in Port and Cream

Serves 4

4 slices French bread,
   diagonally sliced
6 T. butter or margarine
4 boneless beef strip
   steaks, cut ½ inch
   thick (about 1½ lb.)
¼ cup Port wine
½ cup whipping cream

Spread bread on both sides with 4 T. butter. In skillet toast bread until golden. Remove to plates. Brown the steaks on both sides in 2 T. butter (10 minutes for medium-rare). Season with salt and pepper. Place steaks atop bread. Add Port to skillet; stir to blend. Add cream; cook and stir until thickened and bubbly. Pour over meat.

Chinese Spiced Beef

Serves 6 to 8

3 lb. roast beef, cooked
   and sliced
1 T. dry Sherry wine
⅓ cup soy sauce
2 T. sugar

Combine all ingredients in skillet, cover and simmer for 3 hours. Stir occasionally. Serve hot with rice.

Chinese Beef and Mushrooms   Serves 4

½ lb. fresh mushrooms,
    sliced
1 lb. steak, sliced
3 T. soy sauce
1 T. cornstarch
1 T. dry Sherry wine
1 tsp. sugar
1 slice ginger root
4 T. oil, divided
½ tsp. salt

Cut beef across the grain in thin slices, about 2 inches long. Mix beef with soy sauce, cornstarch, sherry, and sugar and set aside. Heat 2 T. oil in skillet. And salt and mushrooms. Stir-fry 2 minutes. Remove from skillet and set aside. Add remaining 2 T. oil to skillet and heat with ginger. Add beef mixture, stirring constantly for 2 minutes until beef is done. Add mushrooms, mix and serve hot.

Creole Liver   Serves 4

4 T. butter or margarine
1 onion, thinly sliced
1 lb. liver
    salt and pepper
    flour
⅓ cup tomato-based chile
    sauce
1 7-oz. can chopped green
    chile
1 cup shredded Jack
    cheese

Melt 2 T. butter in skillet. Add onion and cook until limp. Remove onion and set aside. Cut liver into serving-size pieces. Melt remaining butter in pan. Season liver with salt and pepper, then dredge in flour. Fry liver in butter until cooked. Transfer liver to warm serving plate. Spread with chile and onion. Sprinkle with cheese. Broil for a few minutes to melt cheese.

Chinese Flank Steak

Serves 4 to 6

1 flank steak
½ cup sugar
½ cup soy sauce
1 clove garlic, minced
   flour
1 egg, well beaten
2 green onions, chopped

Cut steak against grain in thin slices. Marinate in soy sauce, sugar and garlic for 30 minutes. Combine egg and onions. Coat with flour and dip in egg mixture. Fry.

Note: This can be covered and kept warm until serving. Try with rice and vegetables.

Favorite Steak

Serves 6

2 lbs. beef sirloin steak,
   1-inch thick
2 T. oil
1 medium onion, sliced
2 T. butter
½ cup dry white wine
1 T. Dijon-style mustard
⅛ tsp. garlic powder, or 1
   garlic clove, minced

In skillet . cook steak 12 minutes in 2 T. cooking oil, turning once. In saucepan cook onion in butter until tender. Stir in wine, mustard and garlic; set aside. Transfer steak to platter; skim excess fat from pan juices. Stir onion-wine mixture into pan juices, scraping pan; heat through. Serve with steak.

Gingered Beef

Serves 4

1 lb. beef sirloin or round
   steak, ½-inch thick
3 T. soy sauce
3 T. cold water
1 T. cornstarch
½ tsp. ground ginger
2 T. cooking oil
2 T. snipped green onion
   tops

Slice beef into ¼-inch wide strips. Blend soy sauce, water, cornstarch and ginger; toss with beef to coat well. Heat oil in heavy skillet or wok. Add beef and stir-fry until brown, 5 to 6 minutes. Sprinkle with onion tops.

Italian Goulash

Serves 4

1 lb. ground beef
1 onion, chopped
1 28-oz. can crushed
    tomatoes
1 garlic clove, minced
1 tsp. dried basil
½ tsp. sugar
1 8-oz. package macaroni,
    freshly cooked
½ cup grated Parmesan
    cheese

Cook beef and onion in skillet until beef is cooked. Discard drippings. Add tomatoes, garlic, basil and sugar. Cover and simmer 25 minutes until thick, stirring occasionally. (Can be prepared 1 day ahead. Cover and refrigerate. Reheat before continuing.) Mix in macaroni. Serve topped with Parmesan.
Note: Kids love this.

Lima Bean-Beef-Ball Casserole

Serves 4

1 10-oz. package frozen
    baby limas, cooked
2 to 3 slices bread, cubed
¼ cup milk
1 tsp. salt
½ tsp. pepper
1 egg
1 clove garlic, crushed
1 lb. lean ground beef
4 T. butter
½ cup water
1 cup sour cream

Preheat oven to 350°. Cook limas, drain. Soak bread in milk. Mix ¾ tsp. salt, ¼ tsp. pepper, egg and garlic; add bread and meat. Shape into small balls and brown in 1 T. butter. Place in casserole. Add ½ cup water to frying pan, pour over beef. Season limas with remaining salt, pepper and butter, then pour over meat in casserole. Bake 30 minutes at 350°. Spread sour cream on top and bake 5 more minutes.
Note: Prepare ahead and bake when needed. Recipe can be doubled. Outstanding dish. Good with salad and bread.

Marinated Flank Steak   Serves 8

1   2-lb. flank steak, scored
1½ cup oil
¾   cup soy sauce
½   cup wine vinegar
⅓   cup lemon juice
¼   cup Worcestershire
      sauce
2   T. Dijon mustard
1   T. pepper
1   sprig parsley
1   clove garlic, minced

Place steak in flat dish. Combine remaining ingredients in blender, blend briefly. Pour over meat. Cover and refrigerate 12 to 24 hours, turning occasionally. Remove meat from marinade and barbecue or broil steak. Cut meat into thin diagonal slices to serve. *Note: Marinade can be saved in refrigerator for another use.*

Microwave Mexican Manicotti   Serves 4

½   lb. ground beef
1   cup refried beans
1   tsp. oregano, crushed
½   tsp. ground cumin
8   manicotti shells
1¼ cups water
1   cup taco sauce
1   8-oz. carton sour cream
¼   cup chopped green
      onions
¼   cup sliced pitted ripe
      olives
½   cup shredded Monterey
      Jack cheese

Combine beef, beans, oregano and cumin; mix. Fill uncooked manicotti shells with meat mixture. Arrange in 10 x 6-inch microwave safe dish. Combine water and taco sauce; pour over manicotti shells. Cover with plastic wrap, vent. Microwave on high 10 minutes, giving dish a half-turn once. Using tongs, turn shells over. Cover and cook on medium for 18 minutes or until pasta is tender, giving dish a half-turn once. Combine sour cream, onion and olives. Spoon down center of casserole; top with cheese. Microwave, uncovered on high 2 minutes or until cheese melts.

Microwave Meat Loaf

Serves 6

1 lb. ground beef
½ lb. ground pork
1 8-oz. can tomato sauce
2 large eggs, beaten
¼ cup rolled oats
¾ cup breadcrumbs
2 T. instant onion
2 T. minced parsley
2 T. Worcestershire sauce
2 tsp. spicy mustard
1 tsp. salt
½ tsp. garlic salt
½ tsp. pepper
½ cup grated Parmesan
   cheese

Combine all ingredients except cheese, blend well. Pack mixture into microwave safe tube pan. Sprinkle with half of the cheese. Microwave uncovered 5 minutes on high. Turn dish and microwave another 5 minutes. Top with remaining cheese, rotate another ½ turn and microwave an additional 5 minutes. Remove from oven, cover and let meat stand 10 minutes before serving.

Simple Sweet and Sour Meatballs

Serves 12

1 - 2 T. margarine
1 medium onion, chopped
1 28-oz. can stewed
   tomatoes
1 6-oz. can frozen
   lemonade, thawed
1½ cups water
½ cup sugar or to taste
2 beef bouillon cubes
3 lb. meatballs, uncooked
   (use favorite recipe)
   freshly cooked rice or
   pasta

Melt margarine in Dutch oven. Add onion and saute until transparent. Add tomatoes, lemonade, water, sugar and bouillon cubes and mix well. Add meatballs and simmer until cooked through, about 1 hour. Drain grease from sauce. Serve meatballs and sauce over rice or pasta. *Note: Freezes well.*

New Mexico Chile con Carne   Serves 4

1 lb. ground beef
1 clove garlic, minced
1 15-oz. can pinto beans
   with chile seasoning
1 envelope dry onion soup
1 cup tomato sauce
¼ tsp. oregano

Brown meat and garlic. Add remaining ingredients. Simmer for 30 minutes. Stir frequently.

Note: This is nice served with a warmed flour tortilla and guacamole salad. Freezes well.

New Mexican Lasagna   Serves 6 to 8

1 lb. ground beef
½ cup chopped onion
1 1¼-oz. envelope dry
   Taco seasoning mix
1 8-oz. can tomato sauce
1 15-oz. can beans with
   Mexican seasoning
1 4-oz. can chopped green
   chile
6 flour tortillas, halved
2 cups shredded Cheddar
   cheese

Preheat oven to 350°. Grease 8 x 12-inch pan. Brown beef and onion in skillet. Drain fat. Stir in seasoning mix, tomato sauce, chile beans and green chile. Layer half of tortillas in bottom of dish. Spread half of meat mixture over and sprinkle with ½ of cheese. Repeat layers. Bake for 30 minutes. Let stand 10 minutes before serving.

Southwest Stroganoff   Serves 8

3 T. cooking oil
1 onion, chopped
1 clove garlic, minced
1 4-oz. can sliced
   mushrooms, drained
2 lbs. beef, cubed
2 cups beef broth
1 4-oz. can diced green
   chile, drained
1 cup sour cream

In skillet heat oil and saute onion, garlic and mushrooms for 2 minutes. Dust beef cubes with seasoned flour. Add beef to skillet and brown. Add broth and chile; cover and simmer for 1½ hours or until tender. Stir in sour cream and heat, do not boil. Serve with pasta.

Steak with Wine and Mushrooms Serves 4

1½ - 2 lb. lean, boneless
   steak, such as sirloin
2 T. butter
1 T. cooking oil
2 garlic cloves, peeled and
    cut in half
  pepper
½ lb. mushrooms, sliced
1 cup red wine

In skillet heat butter and oil. Add garlic. Sprinkle meat with pepper and place in skillet. For medium-rare, cook 7 minutes; turn, cook 2 minutes and add mushrooms. Cook 5 minutes more, stirring mushrooms several times. Remove steak and keep warm. Pour wine into skillet and stir to loosen browned particles from pan. Mash garlic to a paste with fork. Increase heat and cook 2 minutes, until liquid is reduced to syrupy consistency. Slice steak thin across the grain. Arrange meat on platter. Spoon mushrooms over or around meat and pour sauce over all.

Note: Easy way to turn plain steak into something special. Recipe is equally good with inch-thick hamburgers. Can be made ahead and kept warm.

Terrific Teriyaki   Serves 4

1½ lb. cooked beef, cubed
¾ cup cooking oil
½ cup honey
½ cup soy sauce
1 T. Worcestershire sauce
½ tsp. minced fresh ginger

In blender, combine all ingredients except meat. Blend. Pour over meat and marinate in refrigerator overnight. In skillet heat all ingredients and serve with rice.

Gourmet Minute Steaks

Serves 4

4 6 to 8-oz. minute steaks
⅓ cup Cognac
1 T. butter
⅔ cup sour cream
   cracked pepper

Sear steaks. Pour Cognac into pan, ignite on steaks and cook 1 minute. Add butter and sour cream. Heat only, do not boil. Top with cracked pepper.

Superb Stew

Serves 8

3 lbs. cubed beef
1 4-oz. can diced green chile
4 slices bacon, chopped
¼ cup butter or margarine
½ cup brown sugar
⅓ cup vinegar
1 tsp. salt
2 bay leaves
1 1-lb. can tomato sauce

Preheat oven to 325°. Combine all ingredients in baking pan. Bake for 2 hours or until meat is tender. Serve with rice, pasta or mashed potatoes.

Tostado Pizza

Serves 6

2 cups biscuit mix
½ cup water
1 lb. ground beef
1 4-oz. can chopped green chile
1½ cups taco sauce
1 15-oz. can refried beans
1 cup grated cheese
1 cup shredded lettuce
1 tomato, chopped
½ cup onion, chopped

Preheat oven to 450°. Grease 12 inch pizza pan. Combine biscuit mix and water. Roll into 14 inch circle. Pat in pan. Brown beef, add chile and taco sauce. Simmer until thick. Spread beans on dough. Top with meat mixture and cheese. Bake for 18 to 20 minutes or until done. Cut into wedges. Serve with lettuce, tomato, onion and extra taco sauce if desired. *Note: Freezes well.*

Tamale Casserole

Serves 6 to 8

1 lb. ground beef
1 onion, chopped
1 29-oz. can whole
    tomatoes
1 10-oz. can enchilada
    sauce
½ cup pitted black olives
1 8-oz. can whole kernel
    corn, drained
1 tsp. oregano, crumbled
    salt to taste
1 cup cornmeal
½ cup water
½ cup shredded Cheddar
    cheese

Preheat oven to 325°. Cook beef and onion until meat is no longer pink, stirring to keep crumbly. Add tomatoes, enchilada sauce, olives, corn, oregano and season to taste with salt. Cover and simmer for 10 minutes. Turn mixture into 2 quart baking dish. Combine cornmeal and water. Spoon over meat mixture. Bake for 50 minutes. Sprinkle cheese over top and bake 10 minutes longer.

Veal Cutlet Parmesan

Serves 4

6 T. olive oil, divided
1 small onion, chopped
1 clove garlic, minced
2 oz. tomato paste
1 cup plus 2 oz. water
1 16-oz. can crushed
    Italian tomatoes
    pinch of sugar
½ tsp. salt
¼ tsp. pepper
¼ tsp. Italian seasoning
1 lb. veal cutlets
¾ cup Italian bread
    crumbs
2 eggs, lightly beaten
¼ cup Parmesan cheese
¾ cup grated Mozzarella
    cheese

In 2 T. olive oil, saute onion and garlic until transparent. Combine tomato paste and water. Add to onion mixture. Add tomatoes, sugar, salt, pepper and Italian seasoning. Bring to boil and simmer for 1½ hours. Preheat oven to 325°. Combine bread crumbs and Parmesan. Dip cutlets in egg, then roll in bread crumb mixture. Brown lightly in 4 T. olive oil. Pour ½ cup sauce on bottom of baking dish. Place cutlets in dish, top with mozzarella. Pour enough sauce to cover cheese. Bake 20 to 30 minutes.

Apricot Game Hens   **Serves 6**

1   cup apricot preserves
⅓   cup dry white wine
¼   cup butter, melted
2   8-oz. packages stuffing
     mix
¾   cup pecans
6   Cornish game hens
½   cup mushrooms, sliced
     and sauteed
     salt and pepper

Preheat oven to 350°. Combine apricots, wine and butter in small bowl. Prepare stuffing mix according to package directions; stir in pecans and sauteed mushrooms. Sprinkle hens with salt and pepper. Fill with stuffing, spooning remainder into baking dish. Truss hens securely. Arrange in roasting pan. Brush each generously with apricot sauce. Bake hens and remaining stuffing 1 hour, basting hens frequently until done. Spoon remaining stuffing onto serving platter and arrange hens on top.
Note: Great Sunday dinner.

Bleu Chicken   **Serves 6**

6   T. butter
6   chicken breast halves,
     skinned
1   pint sour cream
8   oz. bleu cheese
1   T. Worcestershire sauce
2   garlic cloves, minced
     parsley

Preheat oven to 350°. Grease 9 x 13-inch baking pan. Melt butter in skillet. Add chicken and brown well, 4 minutes per side. Transfer to baking pan. Combine sour cream, bleu cheese, Worcestershire and garlic. Spoon mixture evenly over chicken. Bake uncovered 50 minutes or until done. Garnish with parsley.
Note: Serve over rice.

Baked Chicken Reuben   Serves 8

8 boneless chicken breast
   halves, skinned
1 16-oz. can sauerkraut
4 slices (4 x 6-inches)
   Swiss Cheese
1 8-oz. bottle Thousand
   Island salad dressing
1 T. chopped parsley

Preheat oven to 375°. In 13 x 9-inch baking pan, arrange chicken in single layer. Rinse sauerkraut with running cold water, then press out excess liquid. Cut sliced cheese in half. Place sauerkraut on chicken and top with a piece of cheese. Pour salad dressing over cheese. Cover pan with foil. Bake 40 minutes or until chicken is done. Garnish with parsley.

Note: Fat and cholesterol are lowered, if you use the new fat free, cholesterol free dressing.

Chicken with Basil Cream Sauce   Serves 4

4 boneless chicken breast
   halves, skinned
¼ cup milk
¼ cup Italian bread
   crumbs
3 T. butter or margarine
1 cup chicken broth
2 cups dry white wine
1 cup whipping cream
½ cup sliced pimentos
½ cup fresh basil
¼ cup Parmesan cheese,
   grated
⅛ tsp. pepper

Dip chicken in milk and then in crumbs to coat. In skillet melt butter and cook chicken about 10 minutes until tender and golden on both sides. Set aside and keep warm. In same pan stir broth and wine heating to boil. Loosen brown bits. Add cream and pimentos. Reduce heat, add basil, Parmesan and pepper. Pour sauce over chicken.

Note: This delicious sauce is rich, a little goes a long way.

Burgundy Chicken

Serves 12

3 T. butter
12 boneless chicken breast
   halves, skinned
1 6-oz. can black pitted
   olives, not drained
1 4-oz. can mushrooms,
   not drained
6 oz. Burgundy wine

In skillet melt butter, brown chicken, add remaining ingredients; cook 20 minutes until chicken is done.
Note: Freezes well. Serve with rice or pasta. This attractive, simple to prepare, delicious dish is a real party winner.

Cheese Crusted Chicken

Serves 4

4 boneless chicken breast
   halves, skinned
1 cups flour
½ tsp. salt
⅛ tsp. nutmeg
⅛ tsp. pepper
1 egg lightly beaten
⅔ cup grated Swiss cheese
½ cup dry bread crumbs
¼ cup butter
1 lemon cut in wedges

Blend flour, salt, nutmeg and pepper. In a separate container, beat egg. Mix cheese and crumbs. Coat chicken with flour, then dip in egg, then in cheese-mixture. Melt butter in skillet. Saute chicken on both sides until fully cooked. Garnish with lemon wedges. Serve hot or cold.

Chicken Diable

Serves 6

½ cup honey
¼ cup prepared mustard
¼ cup butter, melted
1 tsp. curry powder
1 tsp. salt
1 chicken, cut-up
   cilantro

Mix honey, mustard, butter, curry and salt. Coat chicken with marinade and place in baking pan skin side up. Bake for 1 hour or until golden, basting twice. Garnish with cilantro.
Note: Easy to prepare in the morning and baked an hour or so prior to arrival of guests.

Chicken with Tarragon Caper Sauce

Serves 4

4 boneless chicken breast
   halves, skinned
3 T. oil
½ cup whipping cream
1 T. drained capers
1 tsp. lemon juice
½ tsp. dry crumbled
   tarragon
1 T. butter

Flatten chicken breasts. Heat oil in skillet. Add chicken, cook until opaque, 5 minutes per side. Set chicken aside; keep warm. Add cream, capers and lemon juice to skillet. Bring to boil. Remove from heat, stir in butter, and juices from chicken plate. Pour sauce over chicken. Serve.

Note: This may be halved or doubled. It is quick and easy.

Chinese Chicken and Mushrooms Serves 2

1 whole chicken breast,
   boned and skinned
1 tsp. dry sherry
2 tsp. cornstarch
1½ tsp. salt
1 4-oz. can mushrooms,
   sliced
1 cup frozen green peas
2 slices ginger root
4 T. cooking oil
¼ cup sliced almonds

Cut chicken into thin slices and mix with sherry, 1 tsp. cornstarch, and 1 tsp. salt. Drain mushrooms and reserve liquid. Mix mushroom liquid with remaining 1 tsp. cornstarch. Heat oil in skillet. Add ginger and chicken. Stir for 2 minutes until the chicken in done. Drain, reserving liquid. Discard ginger. Return chicken liquid to skillet and add mushrooms and ½ tsp. salt. Heat and stir for 30 seconds. Add peas, stirring constantly for 1 minute. Add cornstarch and chicken. When the liquid thickens, serve topped with almonds.

Chicken Tetrazzini   Serves 4

2 T. butter
¼ cup chopped onions
1 10¾-oz. creamy chicken
   and mushroom soup
½ cup water
¼ cup Parmesan cheese,
   grated
1 T. Sherry wine
1 cup cooked, cubed
   chicken
2 T. chopped pimento
1 T. parsley

Melt butter in medium pan over medium heat. Add onions and mushrooms, and saute until tender. Add soup, water, cheese and sherry, stirring occasionally until cheese melts. Add remaining ingredients and heat through. Serve with spaghetti.
Note: This is a good way to use up leftover cooked chicken or turkey.

Chinese Chicken   Serves 4

2½ lb. chicken pieces
    seasoned flour
    cooking oil
2   T. sake
4   T. soy sauce
½   cup water
3   slices ginger, chopped
3   green onions, sliced
1   tsp. sugar

Coat chicken with flour and fry until golden. Drain oil and add remaining ingredients. Cover and cook 20 minutes until done. Turn pieces to cook evenly, and stir to prevent burning.

Duck-Glazed Chicken   Serves 8 to 10

6 lb. chicken parts
1 8-oz. jar apricot jam
2 envelopes dry onion
   soup mix
1 8-oz. bottle Russian
   dressing

Preheat oven to 350°. Line 9 x 13 inch baking dish with foil (that is a MUST). Mix jam, onion soup mix and dressing. Pour over chicken. Bake for 1 hour or till done.

Chicken in Sour Cream

Serves 4

1 broiler chicken,
    quartered
3 T. butter
1 onion, chopped
½ cup dry white wine
3 sprigs parsley
⅛ tsp. basil
⅛ tsp. thyme
    salt and pepper to taste
½ lb. whole mushrooms
½ pint sour cream

Brown chicken and onions in butter. Add wine, parsley, basil, thyme, salt and pepper. Cover and simmer for 1 hour. During last ½ hour, add mushrooms. Refrigerate or freeze. When ready to serve, reheat and add sour cream. Heat but do NOT boil.

Note: Festive dish that can be made ahead; heat and add the sour cream to serve. Good with rice, pasta, or potatoes.

Easy Chicken Cordon Bleu

Serves 8

2 sheets Pepperidge Farm
    Puff Pastry
8 boneless chicken breast
    halves, skinned
¼ tsp. poultry seasoning
3 T. butter
8 slices boiled ham
8 slices tomato
8 slices Swiss cheese
8 whole mushrooms

Preheat oven to 350°. Thaw pastry. Season chicken with poultry seasoning. Saute in butter one minute on each side. Drain, set aside. Cut pastry into 4 squares. On a floured board, roll out pastry squares ⅛-inch thick. Place chicken, ham, tomato, cheese and mushroom on each square; enclose and seal edges. Place on ungreased baking sheet. Bake for 20 minutes or until golden and chicken is done.

Note: Very festive. Make day before, refrigerate covered, and bake before serving.

Creamy Swiss Chicken Breasts   Serves 8

8 chicken breast halves, skinned and boned
8 4 x 4-inch slices Swiss cheese
1 10¾-oz. cans cream of mushroom soup, undiluted
½ cup white wine
1 cup herb-seasoned stuffing mix
3 T. butter

Preheat oven to 350°. Arrange chicken in a lightly greased 9 x 13-inch baking dish. Top with cheese slices. Combine soup and wine. Mix well. Spoon sauce over chicken and sprinkle with stuffing mix. Drizzle butter over crumbs. Bake for 45 minutes.

Note: An easy festive dish.

Crocked Chicken   Serves 6

1 whole chicken
¼ cup butter or margarine
4 T. lemon juice
1 tsp. salt
¼ tsp. pepper
1 tsp. garlic salt
1 tsp. celery salt
1 tsp. dry mustard
1 tsp. paprika
¼ cup grated Parmesan

Combine all ingredients in crockpot. Cover and cook on low 8 to 10 hours.

Note: Put this on in the morning and dinner will be ready when you get home. Serve with rice or pasta.

Parmesan Chicken   Serves 8

8 chicken breast halves, skinned and boned
1 egg, beaten
1 cup bread crumbs
½ cup cooking oil
1 cup spaghetti sauce
⅔ cup mozzarella cheese
⅓ cup Parmesan cheese

Preheat oven to 350°. Pound chicken slightly. Dip in egg then in breadcrumbs; brown in oil. Place in baking dish. Pour sauce on chicken; top with cheeses. Bake 30 min.

Note: Serve with spaghetti, garlic bread, and a green salad.

Phyllo Chicken

Serves 16

1½ cup butter or margarine
2 cups chopped celery
3 medium onion, chopped
1 cup chicken broth
2 T. chopped parsley
¼ tsp. nutmeg
   salt and pepper
3 eggs
20 sheets phyllo
SAUCE:
4 T. butter
5 T. flour
2½ cups chicken broth
1 tsp. salt
¼ cup lemon juice
3 beaten egg yolks

Preheat oven to 350°. Saute celery and onion in ½ cup butter until tender. Add chicken and 1 cup of broth. Cook until liquid is absorbed. Add parsley, nutmeg, salt and pepper to taste; cool. Beat eggs until frothy. Fold eggs into chicken mixture and mix well. Melt 1 cup butter. Brush 5 sheets of phyllo with butter and stack. Spread ¼ of the chicken on the pastry and carefully roll up jelly roll style. Seal ends of rolls. Repeat, make 4 rolls. Place on baking sheets, seam down, brush with butter, bake 40 minutes, until brown and crisp. FOR SAUCE: Melt butter; add flour and stir. Gradually add broth and salt. Stir and cook until bubbly and thick. Mix half of sauce with yolks and lemon juice. Return to remaining sauce, heat thoroughly while stirring constantly. Serve over chicken rolls.

Note: Rolls may be frozen before or after baking. Do not top with sauce if freezing.

Easy Chicken

Serves 8

8 chicken breast halves,
   skinned
   seasoned flour
¼ cup oil
¼ cup chopped onion
3 T. white wine vinegar
3 T. Worcestershire sauce
¾ cup Sauterne wine
1 4-oz. can diced green
   chile

Dust chicken with flour and brown in oil. Combine remaining ingredients and pour over chicken. Cover and simmer 45 minutes until tender. Serve with rice.

Healthy Baked Chicken

Serves 8

8 chicken breast halves,
   skinned
¼ cup oil
1 cup corn flake crumbs
1 tsp. seasoned salt

Preheat oven to 350°. Dip chicken in oil, then in crumbs. Place in single layer on cookie sheet. Sprinkle with seasoned salt. Bake 45 minutes or until done.
Note: Quick, easy entree for those watching cholesterol. Variation: For Healthy Baked Fish, substitute fish for chicken. Adjust baking time.

Quick Mexican Chicken

Serves 4

2 T. butter
1 lb. boneless chicken
1 cup taco sauce
1 cup diced green chile
¼ tsp. garlic salt

Melt butter and saute chicken. Add remaining ingredients and heat until chicken is done, about 10 minutes.
Note: Good served with rice. Freezes well.

French Marinated Chicken

Serves 12

¼ lb. butter
1 clove garlic, minced
2 T. parsley
2 T. brown sugar
1 cup Sauterne
1 T. seasoned salt
12 chicken breast halves, skinned
½ tsp. black pepper
1 tsp. paprika

Melt butter in 9 x 13-inch baking pan. Add garlic, parsley, sugar, Sauterne, and seasoned salt. Mix. Season chicken with pepper and paprika. Place in pan, marinate overnight, covered, in refrigerator. Preheat oven to 350°. Bake uncovered, in marinade for 1 hour, turning chicken after 30 minutes.

Note: Make ahead party dish. Serve with rice pilaf or buttered chicken.

Italiano Stir-Fry

Serves 4

3 T. olive oil
1 clove garlic, minced
2 chicken breasts skinned, boned and cut into 1-inch squares
1 cup fresh, or frozen and thawed Italian green beans
½ cup chopped bell pepper
¼ cup chopped green onion
½ tsp. salt
4 tomatoes, quartered
4 anchovies, mashed
2 T. diced pimento
1 T. capers, drained
2 T. lemon juice
1 tsp. ground red pepper

Place skillet over high heat for 30 seconds. Add oil and garlic and stir-fry 10 seconds. Add chicken, beans, bell pepper, onion and salt; continue stirring until chicken is cooked through, about 3 minutes. Add tomatoes, anchovies, pimento and capers and stir-fry 1 minute. Sprinkle with lemon juice and mix thoroughly. Place on serving platter and sprinkle with ground red pepper.

Hidecki Chicken   Serves 6

6 halved chicken breasts,
   skinned
½ cup butter or margarine
4 T. lemon juice
1 cup grated Parmesan
   cheese
¼ tsp. garlic powder
3 tomatoes

Preheat oven to 350°. Melt butter in casserole; add garlic powder. Dip chicken in butter, then in cheese and put back in casserole. Squeeze 2 T. lemon juice over chicken; quarter tomatoes and place around chicken pieces. Bake one hour. Top with remaining 2 T. lemon juice. Save juices and serve with chicken.
Note: Rice is good with this.

Italian Chicken Patties   Serves 8 to 10

6 eggs, beaten
2 cups grated Parmesan
   cheese (8-oz.)
½ cup bread crumbs
2 lb. ground chicken
½ cup chopped onion
3 T. butter or margarine
4 cups spaghetti sauce
2 cups shredded
   mozzarella cheese

Preheat oven to 350°. Combine eggs, Parmesan, crumbs and chicken. Mix well. Shape mixture into sixteen ¾ inch patties. In skillet cook patties in butter 3 minutes per side until browned. Drain, arrange in two baking dishes. Spoon spaghetti sauce over patties and top with mozzarella. Bake uncovered for 25 minutes or until hot.
Note: Bake both casseroles. Eat one and freeze one. Reheat frozen dish in microwave. Turkey or beef may be substituted for ground chicken.

King Ranch Chicken, New Mexico Style

Serves 8

2   cups diced, cooked chicken
12 corn tortillas
2   cups grated Cheddar cheese
1   large onion, chopped
1   10¾-oz. can cream of chicken soup
1   4-oz. can mushrooms, drained
1   12-oz. can tomatoes and green chile
½   cup chicken broth
1   4-oz. can diced green chile

Preheat oven to 350°. Grease 10 inch square casserole. Quarter tortillas. Mix soup, broth, mushrooms, tomatoes and green chile and cubed chicken (it looks terrible). Layer tortillas, chicken mixture, onions and cheese until all ingredients are used, ending with cheese. Bake 1 hour.

Note: Freezes well.

Lemon Chicken Delight   **Serves 8**

¾   cup butter or margarine
½   cup lemon juice
⅓   cup water
1   tsp. paprika
⅛   tsp. cayenne pepper
2   T. soy sauce
1   tsp. honey
1   tsp. Dijon mustard
2   cloves garlic, minced
4   lb. boneless chicken, skinned

In pan stir all ingredients except chicken. Heat until butter melts. Place chicken in container. Pour marinade over chicken. Refrigerate overnight. Cook chicken and marinade uncovered in skillet 45 minutes or until chicken is done, turning pieces over after 20 minutes. Serve with pasta or rice.

Saucy Chicken

Serves 4

6 chicken breast halves, skinned and boned
⅓ cup dry Sherry wine
¼ cup butter or margarine
1 cup sliced fresh mushrooms
½ cup half and half
2 egg yolks
¼ tsp. salt
  paprika

Cook chicken, covered, in Sherry and butter over medium heat until tender, about 25 minutes. Add mushrooms; cook 3 minutes. Place chicken on warm platter. Beat cream, yolks and ¼ tsp. salt just until blended; add to cooking liquid. Cook and stir until thick. Serve over chicken; sprinkle with paprika.

Savory Low Fat Chicken

Serves 6

6 skinless chicken breast halves
⅓ cup flour
1 tsp. salt
⅛ tsp. pepper
¼ tsp. paprika
2 T. oil
1 medium onion, thinly sliced
¼ cup dry sherry
½ cup water
¼ cup low fat mayonnaise
½ cup nonfat yogurt
2 T. minced parsley

Dust chicken with flour that has been seasoned with salt, pepper and paprika. Put oil in skillet, add chicken and brown on both sides. Top with onion, add sherry and water. Cover and simmer until tender, about 45 minutes. Remove chicken and keep warm. Over low heat add mayonnaise and yogurt to liquid in skillet, blend until smooth. Heat through but do not boil. Add parsley and additional seasoning if desired. Pour over chicken and serve.

Sesame Chicken

Serves 6 to 8

2 T. margarine
1 T. oil
3 lb. chicken, skinned and cut into parts
⅓ cup flour, seasoned with salt and pepper
¼ cup sesame seeds
3 T. minced green onions
½ cup dry white wine
1 T. lemon juice

Preheat oven to 375°. Melt margarine in baking pan. Coat chicken with oil, then roll in flour and arrange in pan. Sprinkle with lemon juice. Bake 30 minutes. Turn chicken, sprinkle with sesame seeds and onions. Pour wine into pan and bake 30 minutes, basting occasionally until done.

Note: Cholesterol watchers, this is for you!

Southwest Chicken

Serves 4

1 lb. boneless chicken
½ cup flour
½ tsp. seasoned salt
7 T. butter or margarine
1 5-oz. jar Old English Cheese Spread
2 T. minced onion
¼ tsp. garlic powder
2 4-oz. cans chopped green chile

Pound chicken thin. Dredge in flour seasoned with seasoned salt. Fry in 3 T. butter until done, 15 minutes. In another pan melt 4 T. butter, cheese spread, onion, garlic and green chile. When chicken is done, top with avocado and tomato slices and pour cheese sauce over all. Serve.

Note: This is a quick, easy, tasty dish. It is good served with rice or flour tortillas.

Oven Baked Chicken   Serves 6

3 - 4 lb. chicken parts
1 cup dried bread crumbs
1 cup Parmesan cheese
2 T. chopped parsley
2 garlic cloves, chopped
  salt and pepper
½ cup melted butter or
  margarine

Preheat oven to 350°. Mix bread crumbs, Parmesan cheese, parsley and garlic. Season with salt and pepper. Put melted butter in a bowl. Dip chicken in butter, then roll in crumb mixture. Place in shallow pan and sprinkle with remaining butter. Bake for 45 minutes.

Wine and Dine Chicken   Serves 8

2 chickens, quartered
  flour
½ cup butter
½ cup onion, minced
1 clove garlic, minced
¼ tsp. crushed rosemary
  leaves
¼ tsp. marjoram
½ cup flour
4 cups chicken broth
1½ cups chopped tomatoes,
  fresh or canned
2 tsp. salt
½ tsp. white pepper
1 whole bay leaf
1 carrot
3 ribs celery
½ lb. fresh mushrooms,
  sliced
½ cup dry white wine

Dust chicken with flour and saute in butter until golden. Remove from pan and set aside. Add onion to pan and saute 2 minutes. Add garlic, rosemary and marjoram and saute 3 more minutes. Blend in ½ cup flour. Gradually whisk in broth, stirring constantly until thickened. Add tomatoes, salt and pepper. Add chicken, bay leaf, carrot and celery to pan and simmer 15 minutes. Add mushrooms and wine. Bring to boil, cover and simmer 30 minutes until chicken is tender. Serve with pasta.

Peachy Chicken

Serves 4

4 boneless chicken breast
  halves, skinned
  salt and pepper to taste
¼ cup butter or margarine
¼ cup green onion,
  minced
1 clove garlic, minced
1 tsp. paprika
1 bunch broccoli, cooked
8 cling peach halves
1 cup sour cream or plain
  yogurt
¼ cup mayonnaise
¼ cup grated Parmesan
  cheese

Preheat oven to 375°. Season chicken with salt and pepper. Saute onions and garlic in butter. Stir in paprika. Coat chicken in butter mixture. Place chicken in baking pan, cover and bake for 35 minutes. Arrange broccoli on one side of pan and peaches on the other. Mix sour cream and mayonnaise and spoon over all. Sprinkle with cheese. Place under broiler 3 minutes just until golden.

Wonderful Chicken

Serves 12

2 cups breadcrumbs
½ cup grated Parmesan
  cheese
⅓ cup chopped parsley
1 3-oz. can French-fried
  onions, crushed
½ cup butter or margarine
2 cloves garlic, crushed
1 tsp. Worcestershire
  sauce
1 tsp. dry mustard
12 chicken breast halves,
  boned and skinned

Preheat oven to 350°. Line a 9 x 13-inch baking dish with foil. Combine breadcrumbs, Parmesan, parsley and onions and mix thoroughly. Melt butter and saute garlic about 1 minute. Remove from heat and stir in Worcestershire and mustard. Dip chicken in butter mixture and then in breadcrumbs, coating well. Arrange in prepared dish. Pour remaining butter mixture over top. Bake until chicken tests done, about 50 minutes. Serve hot.

Braised Turkey Breast Cordon Bleu

Serves 12

2 T. vegetable oil
2 T. butter
1 4 lb. turkey breast
1 large onion, chopped
3 stalks celery, chopped
1 tsp. chicken bouillon
½ tsp. salt
¼ tsp. pepper
¼ tsp. leaf thyme, crushed
½ cup water
5 T. flour
1 cup light cream
¾ lb. thinly sliced
   Canadian bacon
½ cup grated Swiss cheese

Heat oil and butter in flame-proof casserole. Brown turkey in casserole and remove. Saute onion, carrots and celery in casserole until golden. Stir in bouillon, salt, pepper, thyme and water; heat to boiling. Return meat to casserole and cover. Bake for 2 hours at 325°, basting often. Remove meat to carving board. Strain cooking liquid into a 4 cup measure, pressing vegetables against sieve to release juice; discard vegetables. Skim off fat. Return 4 T. of fat to casserole and stir in flour. Heat until bubbly, gradually adding 2 cups of the cooking liquid and cream. Cook, stirring until sauce thickens and bubbles 1 minute. Carve turkey meat in one piece from each side of bone. Slice crosswise into ¼-inch thick slices. Arrange slices alternating with slices of canadian bacon on breast bone in shallow baking dish. Stir cheese into sauce; pour over meat. Refrigerate until ready to bake. About 30 minutes before serving, place dish in 350 degree preheated oven for 30 minutes.

Artichoke and Seafood Casserole

Serves 8

4 T. butter
2 T. chopped shallots
1 clove garlic, chopped
½ lb. mushrooms, sliced
¼ cup flour
1 cup milk
⅔ cup dry white wine
1½ cups Swiss cheese,
  grated
  salt and pepper to taste
1 tsp. dry dill weed
1 lb. shrimp, cooked
1 lb. lump crab meat
1 10-oz. package frozen
  artichoke hearts,
  cooked and drained
3 T. buttered soft bread
  crumbs

Preheat oven to 375°. Melt butter in skillet; saute shallots and garlic until tender. Add mushrooms and cook for two minutes longer. Sprinkle with flour; stir and cook for one minute. Gradually stir in milk, wine, and stock. Bring to boil, stirring until thick. Remove from heat and stir in one cup cheese until it melts. Add salt, pepper and dill. Stir in shrimp, crab and artichoke hearts. Place in buttered casserole. Sprinkle with remaining cheese and bread crumbs. Bake 25 minutes.

Baked Halibut with Olives and Scallions

Serves 4 to 6

½ cup green olives,
  chopped
½ cup black olives,
  chopped
⅔ cup fresh parsley,
  minced
2 T. dill
½ cup scallions, chopped
1 large jalapeno, minced
¼ cup lemon juice
¼ cup olive oil
1½ lb. halibut fillets
1 cup tomato sauce

Preheat oven to 400°. Lightly grease baking pan. Combine olives, parsley, dill, scallions, jalapeno, lemon juice and olive oil. Place halibut in baking dish. Divide olive mixture among fillets. Pour tomato sauce in baking pan. Bake for 15 minutes or until fish is firm and cooked through. Transfer fish to serving platter, top with sauce and serve hot.

Basil Shrimp

Serves 2

10 oz. jumbo shrimp
 2 T. olive oil
 2 T. shallots, chopped
 1 clove garlic, minced
 ¼ cup sun dried tomatoes,
      chopped
 ⅔ cup dry Vermouth
 1 cup whipping cream
 ¼ tsp. dried thyme
 ¼ tsp. sugar
 2 tsp. basil
     salt and pepper

Saute shrimp in hot oil, 1 minute or until cooked through; remove and keep warm. Saute garlic, shallots and tomatoes in remaining oil until wilted. Stir in Vermouth; simmer until syrupy. Add cream, thyme and sugar, cook until reduced and thickened. Stir in shrimp and basil; season to taste and serve. *Note: This is quick and easy. Goes well with pasta. Serves 5 as an appetizer.*

Crab and Artichoke

Serves 8

 3 T. butter
 3 T. flour
1½ cups milk
 1 tsp. salt
 ⅛ tsp. pepper
 1 tsp. Worcestershire
      sauce
 ⅓ cup grated Parmesan
      cheese
 ½ tsp. mustard
 4 hard-boiled eggs,
      quartered
 1 16-oz. can artichoke
      hearts, drained and
      quartered
 2 cups crab meat
     grated Parmesan cheese
     paprika

Preheat oven to 350°. Melt butter in pan and stir in flour to make a roux. Add milk, salt, pepper, Worcestershire, and mustard, stirring constantly until thick. Add ⅓ cup Parmesan. Mix eggs, artichokes and crab, and place in buttered 2-quart casserole. Cover with sauce, sprinkle with additional cheese and paprika. Bake for 30 minutes.

Crab Enchiladas with Chile Sauce

Serves 6

3   4-oz. cans green chile
1½ cups butter or
       margarine
½   cup diced onion
1   tsp. dry rosemary
½   tsp. minced garlic
1   cup dry white wine
2   cups whipping cream
½   tsp. cornstarch
       dissolved in 2 tsp.
       water
¾   lb. mushrooms
2   tsp. minced shallots
½   cup dry vermouth
1   lb. cooked crabmeat,
       drained
     Chile Sauce
¼   cup snipped chives
1½ tsp. pepper
12 blue or yellow corn
       tortillas

Puree chile in blender until smooth. Melt ½ cup butter in skillet. Add chile paste, onion, rosemary, pepper, shallot and garlic; stir 2 minutes. Add wine and boil until reduced by half. Add cream and boil 10 minutes stirring occasionally. Stir in cornstarch mixture and boil 1 minute, stirring constantly. Slice mushrooms. Melt ½ cup butter in skillet. Add mushrooms and shallots; cook 10 minutes until tender. Add vermouth and bring to boil. Reduce heat and simmer 6 minutes until all liquid is gone, stirring occasionally. Melt ½ cup butter in skillet. Add crab and stir until heated through. Combine with mushrooms. Mix in ¾ cup chile sauce, chives and pepper; bring to boil, stirring constantly. Preheat oven to 350°. Stack tortillas and wrap in foil. Bake 10 minutes until heated through. Divide filling among tortillas. Fold tortillas, envelope style and place seam side down on plates. Top with remaining sauce and serve.

Crunchy Fish   Serves 4

1 lb. fish fillets, such as
   flounder or sole
¼ cup lemon juice
½ cup finely chopped
   walnuts
3 T. butter or margarine

Dip fish in lemon juice then into nuts. Saute in butter until golden brown. about 4 minutes per side.

Note: The nuts add a delightful crunch to the fillets.

Deviled Lobster Tails   Serves 6

4 lobster tails
3 tsp. salt
1 tsp. cayenne pepper
10 whole cloves
½ lemon
1 small onion
1 tsp. peppercorns
¼ cup butter
½ cup chopped celery
½ cup chopped onion
½ cup chopped bell pepper
¼ cup chopped parsley
2 hard cooked eggs
1 raw egg
6 drops Tabasco
2 cups buttered bread
   crumbs, divided
   milk
   salt and pepper
6 bowls of melted butter

Fill large pot with water. Add salt, cayenne, garlic, lemon, onion and peppercorns. Bring to boil and drop in lobster tails. Keep at full boil for 20 minutes. Remove tails from water and split in half. Remove meat and save 6 half shells. Saute the chopped vegetables in ¼ cup butter until onion is transparent. Break lobster meat into chunks and put in bowl. Add remaining ingredients, except melted butter and half the bread crumbs, using just enough milk to make the mixture hold together. Fill shells with the mixture, piling high, and top with the rest of the bread crumbs. Bake in 350 degree oven 20 minutes until brown. Serve at once with melted butter for each portion.

Note: This can be prepared early in the day, covered and refrigerated.

Cantonese Shrimp   Serves 6

1 lb. shrimp, shelled
2 T. oil
1 clove garlic, minced
¼ cup green onion, sliced
½ tsp. ginger root, minced
½ tsp. salt
¼ tsp. pepper
1 10½-oz. can chicken
    broth
1 6-oz. package frozen
    snow peas, thawed
1 T. cornstarch mixed
    with 1 T. water

Heat oil in skillet and saute shrimp, garlic and onions for 5 minutes. Add ginger, salt, pepper, chicken broth and peas. Simmer 6 minutes. Stir cornstarch mixture into shrimp mixture and simmer for 1 minute longer. Serve over hot rice.

Fancy Fillet of Sole   Serves 4

2 T. butter or margarine
2 T. flour
1 cup milk
¼ tsp. seasoned salt
⅛ tsp. pepper
    dash nutmeg
1 T. Sherry wine
4 pieces of foil
1 4½-oz. can shrimp,
    drained
1 3-oz. can sliced
    mushrooms, drained
½ tsp. Worcestershire
    sauce
¼ tsp. paprika
4 frozen sole fillets,
    thawed
1 T. minced parsley

Preheat oven to 400°. In saucepan melt butter, add flour and stir until smooth. Gradually add milk, stirring constantly to make smooth white sauce. Heat sauce, stirring constantly until it thickens. Add salt, pepper, nutmeg and sherry. Blend well and remove from heat. Add shrimp, mushrooms, Worcestershire and paprika to white sauce. On each piece of foil place one sole fillet; top each with ¼ of the shrimp mixture, garnish with parsley. Fold foil and seal. Bake for 20 minutes.

Fettucine with Clam Sauce   Serves 3

1   1-oz. package dry Ranch Salad dressing mix
¾   cup milk
½   cup mayonnaise
¼   cup melted butter or margarine
1   10-oz. can whole baby clams, drained
½   cup chopped, pitted ripe olives - optional
4   oz. spinach fettucine, cooked and drained
2   T. chopped fresh parsley

Combine dressing mix, milk and mayonnaise. Let stand 30 minutes to thicken. Combine melted butter, clams and olives. Heat through. Toss fettucine with dressing mix, parsley and clam mixture. Serve warm.
Note: Recipe can be doubled.

Fillet of Sole Stir-Fry   Serves 4

1   lb. sole fillets, cut into 1½-inch squares
½   tsp. salt
¼   tsp. white pepper
2   T. flour
1   T. lemon juice
1   T. sugar
1   T. dry vermouth
2   T. oil
1   celery stalk, minced

Sprinkle fish with salt and pepper. Dust with flour. Combine lemon juice, sugar and wine in small saucepan over low heat and cook until sugar is dissolved and sauce is reduced by half. Remove sauce from heat and set aside; keep warm. Place large skillet over high heat. Add oil. Add celery and stir-fry 2 minutes. Add fish and continue stirring until it is firm and white, about 3 minutes. Turn onto platter. Pour lemon sauce over and serve.

Dilled Salmon

Serves 4

1 medium onion, sliced
1 tsp. chicken bouillon
1½ cups water
1 T. lemon juice
4 salmon steaks
2 T. butter or margarine
1 T. chopped onion
2 T. flour
1 tsp. salt
1 tsp. dill weed
⅛ tsp. pepper
1½ cups milk

Combine the sliced onion, bouillon, water and lemon juice in skillet. Heat to boiling. Add salmon; cover and simmer 10 minutes or until fish flakes easily. In saucepan, cook chopped onion in butter until tender; stir in flour, salt, dill and pepper. Add milk, mixing well. Heat, stirring constantly until mixture boils and thickens. Pour sauce over hot salmon to serve.

Fish with Capers

Serves 4 to 5

¼ cup butter or margarine
1 tsp. grated lemon peel
1½ lb. skinless white-flesh
        fish fillets, about 1-
        inch thick
1 cup seasoned bread
        crumbs
2 T. drained capers
        lemon wedges
        salt and pepper

Preheat oven to 425°. Place butter in 13 x 9-inch baking pan and set in oven 5 minutes until melted. Stir in lemon. Turn fillets in butter, then in crumbs, to coat all sides. Arrange fillets in a single layer in baking pan. Bake, uncovered 15 minutes, until crumbs are golden and fish is opaque but still moist. With spatula, carefully transfer fish to platter. Top with capers, lemon wedges, salt and pepper.

Happy Dieter's Haddock   Serves 6

2 lbs. haddock fillets,
    fresh or frozen
    (thawed)
1½ cups fresh tomatoes,
    chopped
½ cup green pepper,
    chopped
⅓ cup lemon juice
1 T. safflower oil
2 tsp. salt
2 tsp. instant minced
    onion
1 tsp. crushed basil leaves
¼ tsp. black pepper
4 drops Tabasco

Preheat oven to 500°. Place fillets in baking dish. Combine remaining ingredients; spoon mixture over fillets. Bake 8 minutes or until fillets are done. Serve.
Note: This tasty dish only has 155 calories and 3 grams fat per serving!

Sauteed Shrimp with Garlic and Herbs
Serves 6

3 lb. large shrimp, peeled
    and deveined
⅓ cup olive oil
6 medium garlic cloves,
    minced
¾ cup dry white wine
3 T. lemon juice
¾ cup butter, cut into ½-
    inch pieces
2 T. chopped parsley
1 T. snipped chives
½ tsp. dried tarragon
    salt and pepper to taste

Heat oil in skillet. Add shrimp and saute 3 minutes until just opaque. Remove with slotted spoon and drain on paper towels. Remove all but 1 T. oil from skillet. Add garlic and stir 30 seconds. Add wine, increase heat and reduce mixture by ⅓. Add lemon juice and return to boil. Remove from heat. Swirl in butter, blending until creamy. Stir in parsley, chives and tarragon. Season with salt and pepper, and additional lemon juice if desired. Arrange shrimp on individual plates. Top with sauce.

Crispy Baked Fish Fillets   Serves 4

1 lb. fish fillets
2 T. oil
⅓ cup corn flake crumbs
¼ tsp. salt
   pepper

Preheat oven to 500°. Place oil in shallow baking sheet. Dip fillets in oil then crumbs. Place in single layer on baking sheet. Season and bake 10 minutes. Do not turn or baste.

Fish Dilly   Serves 4

1 20-oz. package frozen, fried, breaded fish portions (8 pieces)
¼ cup sour cream
2 T. lemon juice
1 T. dried parsley flakes
2 tsp. instant minced onion
½ tsp. dried dill weed, crushed

Preheat oven to 500°. Place fish on baking sheet and bake for 10 minutes until heated through. In bowl combine sour cream, lemon juice, parsley, onion and dill. To serve, spoon sour cream mixture over fish or serve separately.

Hurry Curry Shrimp   Serves 4

¼ cup butter or margarine
¾ cup chopped onion
2 garlic cloves, minced
3 T. flour
2 T. curry powder
½ tsp. ground ginger
1 cup chicken broth
1 cup whipping cream
1 lb. cooked medium shrimp, shelled
2 T. lemon juice
   freshly cooked rice

Melt butter in large skillet and add onion and garlic. Saute until translucent. Stir in flour, curry and ginger and cook 3 minutes. Add broth and cream. Stir until thickened, about 5 minutes. Add shrimp and lemon juice and cook until heated through, about 2 minutes. Serve shrimp over rice.

Great Southwestern Shrimp   Serves 6

½ cup butter or margarine
½ cup taco or picante
      sauce
¼ cup chopped onion
¼ cup chopped celery
2 lb. shrimp, shelled,
      deveined and
      seasoned with salt,
      pepper and cayenne
¼ cup dry white wine
¼ cup chopped parsley
2 T. minced shallot

Melt butter in large skillet over medium heat. Add taco sauce, onion and celery and saute until vegetables are tender. Add shrimp and wine and saute until shrimp is done, about 5 minutes. Stir in parsley and shallots. Serve over rice.

Sole in Almond Shrimp Sauce   Serves 4

1 lb. sole fillets
1 cup dry white wine
3 oz. baby shrimp
4 T. butter
2 T. flour
½ cup half and half
¼ tsp. salt
      dash pepper
⅓ cup slivered almonds,
      toasted

Preheat oven to 350°. Poach fillets in wine 15 minutes or until fish flakes easily. Do not overcook. Reserve ¼ cup shrimp; mash remaining with 2 T. butter; set aside. In small saucepan, heat remaining 2 T. butter. Add flour; cook 3 minutes. Gradually stir in half and half. Cook and stir until sauce begins to thicken. Stir in ½ cup of fish cooking liquid; continue cooking, and stirring until sauce boils. Reduce heat, add shrimp-butter, salt and pepper; stir until butter melts. Stir in ¼ cup of the almonds. Arrange fillets on serving platter. Pour sauce over sole; garnish with rest of shrimp and almonds.

Microwave Mexican Shrimp Serves 4

1 large onion, chopped
1 4-oz. can diced green
   chile, drained
2 T. oil
2 garlic cloves, minced
1 8-oz. can tomato sauce
¼ cup dry white wine
½ tsp. dried oregano
½ tsp. salt
¼ tsp. ground cumin
   dash Tabasco sauce
1 lb. jumbo shrimp,
   shelled and deveined
2 T. chopped parsley

Combine onion, chile, oil and garlic in microwave safe dish. Microwave on high for 3 minutes. Stir in tomato sauce, wine, oregano, salt, cumin and Tabasco. Cover and microwave on high 5 minutes. Add shrimp and toss lightly to coat with sauce. Microwave on high until shrimp just turn pink, about 5 to 7 minutes. Garnish with parsley.
Note: Accompany this quick dish with hot rice or noodles.

New Mexico Snapper Serves 4

1 lb. red snapper fillets
1 8-oz. can tomato sauce
1 4-oz. can diced green
   chile
¼ tsp. garlic salt

Combine all ingredients and microwave on high until fish is done, about 8 minutes.

Spicy Shrimp Serves 8

1 cup Italian salad
   dressing
½ cup butter, melted
2 T. lemon juice
2 T. black pepper
4 lb. shrimp, in shell,
   heads removed

Preheat oven to 450°. Combine all ingredients and bake for 20 minutes or until shrimp are done. Serve shrimp passing sauce separately.
Note: Simple but excellent.

SOUTHWEST SEASONS SOUTHWEST SEASONS SOUTHWEST SEASONS SOUTHWEST SEASONS SOUTHWEST

Parmesan Fried Fish   Serves 4

1 lb. fish fillets
¼ cup flour
   dash garlic salt
1 beaten egg
¼ cup milk
½ cup (14 crackers)
       saltine cracker
       crumbs
2 T. Parmesan cheese
2 T. parsley
½ cup oil for frying

Combine flour and garlic salt, set aside. Blend egg and milk, set aside. Combine crumbs, Parmesan and parsley. Coat fish with flour. Dip in egg then coat with crumbs. In skillet add fish in a single layer to hot oil. Fry over medium heat for 5 minutes per side or until fish browns and is cooked through. Drain on paper towels and serve.

Sherried Scallops   Serves 4

2 T. butter
2 garlic cloves, minced
   pinch of tarragon
   pinch of oregano
1 lb. sea scallops, cut into
       1-inch pieces
   pinch of paprika
   salt and pepper to taste
1 T. lemon juice
2 T. sherry

Melt butter in skillet. Stir in garlic, tarragon and oregano. Add scallops and season with paprika, salt and pepper. Squeeze lemon juice over scallops and saute 5 minutes until scallops turn opaque. Taste and adjust seasoning, increase heat and add sherry. Continue cooking, stirring constantly, until liquid has almost evaporated. Transfer scallops to shallow dish. Sprinkle additional paprika over top and garnish with parsley and lemon slice.
Note: Equally tasty made with shrimp.

Scallop Creole   Serves 4

½ cup onion, chopped
½ cup celery, chopped
1 clove garlic, minced
3 T. oil
1 16-oz. can tomatoes,
        chopped
1 8-oz. can tomato sauce
1½ tsp. salt
¼ tsp. sugar
½ tsp. chili powder
1 T. Worcestershire sauce
¼ tsp. Tabasco
1 T. cornstarch
2 T. cold water
1 lb. scallops
½ cup green pepper,
        chopped

Saute onion, celery, and garlic in oil 5 minutes or until tender. Add tomatoes, tomato sauce and seasonings. Simmer uncovered for 45 minutes. Mix cornstarch and water. Add to sauce and stir until smooth and thick. Add scallops and green pepper. Simmer covered another 10 minutes. Serve with rice.

Stroganoff with Clams   Serves 6

½ cup butter or margarine
1 T. oil
4 cloves garlic, minced
1 T. Worcestershire sauce
2 tsp. seasoned salt
¼ cup minced onion
1 cup chopped parsley
1 lb. mushrooms, sliced
1 4-oz. can diced green
        chile
2 10-oz. cans chopped
        clams, drained
1 cup sour cream

Heat butter and oil in skillet; saute garlic, Worcestershire, seasoned salt and onion for 3 minutes. Stir in parsley, mushrooms and chile. Simmer 20 minutes. Stir in clams, cover and simmer 30 minutes. Stir in sour cream and heat through, but do not boil. Serve with rice or pasta.

SOUTHWEST SEASONS SOUTHWEST SEASONS SOUTHWEST SEASONS SOUTHWEST SEASONS SOUTHWEST

Special Shrimp   **Serves 6**

1½ lb. shrimp
 ½ cup butter
 1 medium onion, chopped
 ½ garlic clove, minced
 1 oz. Sherry wine
 ½ lb. fresh mushrooms,
       sliced
 1 lb. tomatoes, skinned
       and diced
 1 cup consomme
    salt and pepper to taste

Shell raw shrimp and cook in butter until done. Add onion, garlic, sherry, mushrooms, tomatoes, consomme, salt and pepper to taste. Simmer for 30 minutes.

Note: This is especially good served over rice as the sauce is delicious.

Tasty Flambe Shrimp   **Serves 4**

 2 stalks celery, sliced
 3 green onions, sliced
 1 clove garlic, minced
 3 T. butter
 ¾ lb. shelled shrimp
 1 7½-oz. can tomatoes
 ¼ tsp. dried basil
 ¼ tsp. salt
    dash pepper
 ¼ cup slivered almonds,
       toasted
 ¼ cup brandy
 2 cups hot cooked rice

In skillet cook celery, onion and garlic in butter until tender. Add shrimp. Continue cooking 3 minutes or until shrimp are pink. Stir in undrained tomatoes, basil, salt and pepper. Stir over low heat for 2 minutes until heated through. Stir in almonds. In separate pan heat brandy just until warm. On serving platter arrange shrimp mixture atop rice. To serve, ignite brandy and pour over shrimp.

Note: Quick and easy for parties. Also good made with boneless chicken.

Swift Scampi

Serves 4

¾ cup butter
¼ cup minced onion
3 garlic cloves, minced
1 T. minced parsley
1 lb. uncooked medium
    shrimp, deveined
¼ cup dry white wine
2 T. lemon juice
    salt and pepper to taste

Melt butter in medium skillet over low heat. Add onion, garlic and parsley and saute until golden; 10 minutes. Add shrimp and stir just until pink. Remove shrimp and place in ovenproof dish. Keep warm. Add wine and lemon juice to skillet and simmer about 2 minutes. Season with salt and pepper and pour over shrimp.
Note: Serve hot over rice.

Simple Summer Shrimp

Serves 6

1 12-oz. can beer
¼ tsp. salt
¼ tsp. celery salt
⅛ tsp. onion powder
1½ lbs. frozen shelled
    shrimp
¼ cup butter or margarine
1 T. lemon juice
½ tsp. dried dill weed,
    crushed

In pan bring beer, salts and onion powder to boil. Add shrimp. Heat to boiling; reduce heat and simmer 2 minutes until shrimp are pink. In microwave melt butter. Stir in lemon juice and dill. Serve hot butter mixture with shrimp.

Shrimp Vesuvius
Serves 10

2 4-oz. cans small shrimp
   or ½ lb. fresh shrimp
½ lb. bay scallops, sliced
½ lb. mozzarella cheese,
   diced
3 T. Worcestershire sauce
1 clove garlic, minced
½ tsp. horseradish
2 T. butter
2 T. flour
½ cup milk
½ cup chicken broth
   Parmesan cheese
   Cognac or Brandy

Preheat oven to 400°. Grease individual oven-proof dishes (shell-shaped are nice if available). Place scallops in dish, arrange shrimp on top place cheese on top of shrimp. Make Bechamel Sauce by melting the butter, add flour and whisk well. Slowly add milk and broth, whisking all the while. Add the Worcestershire, garlic and horseradish until smooth. Pour Bechamel Sauce over cheese and sprinkle with Parmesan. Bake uncovered 20 minutes or until bubbly on top. Serve hot.

Note: This party do-ahead dish can be doubled. Can be frozen until serving time and heated in oven for 30 minutes. For "Vesuvius" effect, warm Brandy, pour on top, and serve flaming. A delicious, beautifully presented entree that your guests will not soon forget.

Flounder Almandine
Serves 4

4 8-oz. flounder fillets
2 T. dry Vermouth
2 T. lemon juice
2 T. butter, softened
⅓ cup slivered almonds,
   toasted

Place fish in microwave-safe pan. Sprinkle wilth Vermouth and lemon juice; dot with butter. Cover and microwave on high for 3 minutes. Top with almonds, rotate, and cook for 3 more minutes.

Cantonese Egg Foo Yung

Serves 4

5   large eggs
½   cup pork, cooked and
      shredded
½   cup celery, minced
1   4-oz. can mushrooms,
      drained and minced
1   cup bean sprouts,
      chopped
¼   cup onion, minced
1½ tsp. salt
1   tsp. dry Sherry wine
⅛   tsp. pepper
4   T. oil
1   14-oz. can chicken broth
1   tsp. ketchup
1   T. soy sauce
2½ T. flour
¼   cup water

Gently mix eggs, meat, celery, mushrooms, bean sprouts, onion, 1 tsp. salt, Sherry and pepper. Heat 4 T. oil in skillet; pour ½ cup of egg mixture into skillet and fry as a pancake, turning over when cooked on one side. Add more oil, if required. Continue with remaining egg mixture. In second pan combine chicken broth, ketchup, soy sauce, and ½ tsp. salt. Combine flour and water. Add flour mixture to chicken broth and cook, stirring constantly until mixture boils and thickens.

Cottage Enchiladas

Serves 6

12 corn tortillas
      cooking oil
1   14-oz. can green chile,
      diced
1   12-oz. carton cream-
      style cottage cheese
1½ cup sour cream
⅛   tsp. black pepper
8   oz. Cheddar cheese, cut
      into 12 strips
1   14-oz. can enchilada
      sauce
½   cup grated Cheddar
      cheese
1   4-oz. can sliced ripe
      olives

Preheat oven to 350°. Dip tortillas in hot oil until limp; drain. Combine cottage cheese, ½ cup sour cream and pepper. Place green chile, 1 strip of cheese and 1 T. cottage cheese mixture on each tortilla. Roll up, and place seam-side down in 12 x 7 x 2-inch baking dish. Mix ½ cup sour cream with enchilada sauce and pour over tortillas. Top with remaining sour cream, grated cheese and olives. Bake for 30 minutes.

Microwave Ham and Cheese   Serves 6 to 8

6 green onions, sliced
1 4-oz. can sliced
   mushrooms, drained
2 T. butter or margarine
1 cup cottage cheese
1 cup sour cream
½ tsp. celery salt
¼ tsp. pepper
8 oz. spaghetti, cooked
   and drained
3 cups cubed cooked ham
1 cup shredded Cheddar
   cheese

In a 12 x 7-inch microwave safe dish, combine onions, mushrooms and butter. Microwave, covered, on high for 3½ minutes, stirring once. Stir in cottage cheese, sour cream, celery salt and pepper. Add spaghetti and ham; mix well. Cover; cook on high for 12 to 14 minutes, giving dish a quarter turn, after 4 and 8 minutes. Sprinkle cheese on top. Cover, let stand 5 minutes to melt cheese.
Note: Family-style dish is hearty, tasty, quick and easy.

Microwave Quiche   Serves 6

2 cups grated Monterey
   Jack cheese
9 strips bacon, crisply
   cooked and crumbled
1 4-oz. can diced green
   chile
3 green onions, thinly
   sliced
1 baked 9-inch deep-dish
   pie shell
1 13-oz. can evaporated
   milk
4 eggs

Combine Jack cheese, bacon, chile and onions in bowl and toss lightly. Sprinkle about ¾ of mixture over pie shell. Microwave milk in measuring cup on high for 2½ minutes. Beat eggs in separate bowl. Add hot milk and beat again. Pour evenly into pie shell. Sprinkle with remaining bacon mixture. Microwave at 60 percent power until center is barely set, about 12 to 15 minutes. Let stand 5 minutes before serving.

Baked Pork Chops   Serves 8

8 pork chops
½ tsp. garlic salt
½ tsp. onion salt
1½ cups graham cracker
    crumbs

Preheat oven to 350°. Season chops with salts. Coat with crumbs and place on baking dish, covered. Bake for 35 minutes.

Chinese Pork and Peas   Serves 2

½ lb. pork, shredded
1 10-oz. package frozen
    green peas
1 tsp. dry Sherry wine
2 tsp. cornstarch
1 T. soy sauce
2 T. oil
1 tsp. salt
1 slice ginger root

Mix pork, Sherry, 1 tsp. cornstarch and soy sauce; set aside. Mix 1 tsp. cornstarch and 2 T. water. Heat oil in pan. Add ginger, salt and pork mixture. Stir for 4 minutes until pork is cooked. Add peas and stir for 3 minutes. Stir in cornstarch mixture until liquid thickens.

New Mexico Green Chile Rellenos
Serves 6 to 8

12-16 whole green chiles,
        canned or frozen
1   lb. Jack cheese, cut in
        thin strips
½ lb. grated Cheddar
        cheese
½ tsp. paprika
5   large eggs
¼ cup flour
1¼ cups milk
½ tsp. salt
½ tsp. black pepper
⅛ tsp. Tabasco

Preheat oven to 350°. Grease 9 x 13-inch baking pan. Clean seeds from chile. Slip strip of Monterey Jack in each chile. Arrange in single layer in pan. Sprinkle with grated cheese and paprika. Beat eggs, add flour, beat until smooth. Add milk, salt, pepper and Tabasco. Mix thoroughly. Pour egg mixture over chile. Bake uncovered 45 minutes or until set.

New Mexican Spaghetti   Serves 4

½ lb. bacon, cut into ¼-
   inch strips
1 small onion, minced
2 garlic cloves, minced
1½ tsp. minced jalapeno
   chile with seeds
⅛ tsp. dried sage
¾ cup dry white wine
3 cups prepared spaghetti
   sauce
1 lb. spaghetti, cooked
1 T. chopped fresh
   parsley
   grated Parmesan cheese

Cook bacon in skillet. Add onion, garlic, jalapeno and sage; saute 3 minutes. Drain grease from skillet. Add wine and boil until liquid is reduced by half, about 2 minutes. Add spaghetti sauce and simmer 5 minutes. Transfer spaghetti to serving dish. Mix parsley into sauce. Pour sauce over pasta and toss to coat. Serve, passing Parmesan separately.
Note: Sauce may be prepared 1 day ahead and refrigerated.

Sauced Chops   Serves 6

2 T. grated Parmesan
   cheese
½ cup bread crumbs
½ tsp. garlic salt
½ tsp. oregano
½ cup butter or
   margarine, melted
6 ½-inch thick pork chops
½ lb. mushrooms, sliced
1 clove garlic, minced
¼ tsp. rosemary
1 cup whipping cream
¼ cup sliced green onions
   salt and pepper to taste

Preheat oven to 375°. Combine cheese, crumbs, garlic salt, and oregano. Dip chops in butter then dust chops with crumbs. Place in baking pan and bake, uncovered for 1 hour or until done. Saute mushrooms, garlic, and rosemary for 5 minutes. Add cream and cook until liquid is reduced to half. Add onions, salt and pepper. Serve with chops.

Pork and Artichokes

Serves 3 to 4

- 2 T. butter
- 2 T. olive oil
- 1 large onion, diced
- 2 cloves garlic, minced
- 2 T. snipped parsley
- 1 T. tomato paste
- 1 cup chicken broth
- 1½ cups diced cooked pork
- 1 6-oz. jar marinated artichoke hearts, undrained
- dash of lemon pepper

Melt butter. Saute onion and garlic in butter and oil. Add remaining ingredients and simmer about 30 minutes. This is nice served with rice or pasta.

Sweet and Sour Mandarin Pork

Serves 6

- 2 cups cubed pork
- 1 T. dry sherry
- 1 T. soy sauce
- 3 T. corn starch
- 2 cups cooking oil
- ⅔ cup sugar
- ¼ cup ketchup
- ⅓ cup pineapple juice
- ½ cup cider vinegar
- 2 T. soy sauce
- 1 clove garlic, minced
- 1 T. cooking oil
- 2 T. corn starch (mix with ⅓ cup water)
- 1 cup pineapple chunks, drained

Heat oil to 350°. Mix pork, sherry, soy sauce, and corn starch. Separate meat and fry in oil 8 minutes until well done and crisp. Drain on paper towels and keep warm. Combine sugar, ketchup, pineapple juice, vinegar and soy sauce and set aside. Heat 1 T. of oil and saute garlic. Add sugar and vinegar mixture carefully. Cook until mixture starts to boil. Stir in cornstarch mixture, stirring constantly until sauce thickens and becomes translucent. Add pineapple chunks first, then the fried pork. Mix to coat. Serve immediately.

Saucy Ham and Potatoes

Serves 3 or 4

2 T. chopped onion
¼ cup butter or margarine
¼ cup flour
1 tsp. salt
½ tsp. dry mustard
   dash pepper
1½ cups milk
2 cups shredded Cheddar
   cheese
½ lb. ham cut in ⅛ inch
   slices
6 cups cooked potato
   slices

Preheat oven to 350°. Lightly grease 2 quart casserole. Saute onion in butter. Blend in flour and seasonings. Gradually add milk. Cook, stirring constantly until thickened. Add 1½ cups cheese, stir until melted. Toss potatoes in cheese sauce. Pour into casserole, reserving 1 cup potato slices. Arrange ham and remaining potato slices on top of casserole. Top with remaining cheese. Bake for 30 minutes.

Pork Chops and Gravy

Serves 4

4 pork chops
3 green onions, chopped
⅓ cup milk
1 10¾-oz. can cream
   mushroom soup

Brown chops well adding onion during last 3 minutes. Thin soup with milk and pour over chops. Simmer 10 minutes.
Note: This is equally good made with beef. Quick family dinner after a long day!

Teriyaki Pork Chops

Serves 8

8 pork chops
1½ cups teriyaki sauce

Marinate chops in sauce overnight in refrigerator. Cook on grill for 15 to 20 minutes on each side or until done.

Kielbasa
Serves 4

4 cups thinly sliced cabbage
1 medium onion, sliced
1 lb. Kielbasa, cut into ½ inch pieces
¾ cup sour cream
2 T. prepared brown mustard
¼ tsp. salt
⅛ tsp. pepper

In large skillet combine cabbage, onion and Kielbasa. Cover and cook over medium heat 15 to 20 minutes, until cabbage and onion are soft and translucent. Stir in sour cream, mustard, salt and pepper. Heat through.

Note: Here's an economical supper. It's simple to make, and tasty too.

Tortilla Roll-Ups
Serves 8

1½ lb. bulk Italian sausage
2 cups cottage cheese
2 T. flour
1 tsp. dried oregano, crushed
1 tsp. dried basil, crushed
¼ tsp. garlic powder
3 cups spaghetti sauce
10 flour tortillas
1½ cups shredded mozzarella cheese

Preheat oven to 375°. In skillet cook sausage until browned; drain off fat. Stir in cottage cheese and flour. Add oregano, basil and garlic powder to spaghetti sauce. Stir ½ cup spaghetti sauce into the sausage mixture. Spoon ⅓ cup meat mixture onto each tortilla; roll up jelly-roll style. Place tortillas, seam side down, in a 13 x 9 x 2-inch baking pan. Pour remaining spaghetti sauce over tortillas. Bake, covered for 35 to 40 minutes. Uncover; sprinkle mozzarella cheese atop. Bake 3 minutes or until cheese melts.

Note: A mild dish that especially appeals to children. Accompany with Spanish rice.

Stuffed Pork Loin

Serves 10

4 lbs. boneless pork loin roast, with pocket for stuffing
1 cup pitted prunes
1 cup dried apricots
½ cup butter, softened
1 clove garlic, minced
salt and pepper to taste
1 T. dried thyme
1 cup Madeira wine
1 T. molasses

Preheat oven to 350°. Push fruit into pocket of roast, alternating prunes and apricots. Set roast in shallow baking pan. Butter the roast and sprinkle it with the spices. Blend wine and molasses and pour over roast. Bake for 1½ hours (20 minutes per lb.), basting twice. Remove from oven, cover and let stand for 15 minutes before serving.

Wine and Pork Chops

Serves 4

1 tsp. sage
1 tsp. rosemary
2 cloves garlic, minced
salt and pepper to taste
4 center-cut pork chops, 1-inch thick
2 T. butter
1 T. oil
¾ cup dry white wine

Combine sage, rosemary, garlic, salt and pepper. Press a little of this mixture into both sides of each pork chop. Melt butter and oil in skillet. Brown chops on both sides. Remove and pour off all but 1 T. of fat from pan. Add ½ cup wine and bring to boil. Return chops to pan. Cover and simmer until chops are tender, about 25 minutes. When ready to serve, remove chops to heated plate. Add remaining ¼ cup wine to skillet and boil down to a syrupy glaze. Pour over pork chops and serve.

Side Dishes

AFTER THE RAIN

The Nambe Valley, starting point of the high road to Taos, winds along Nambe Creek toward the ancient villages of Chimayo, Cordova and Truchas, New Mexico. This magnificent drive, bordered by old cottonwoods and restored adobe haciendas, toward badlands of beautifully colored cliffs is an unforgettable experience.

Baked Honey Tomatoes

Serves 8

8   ripe medium tomatoes
½   cup coarse bread
      crumbs, unseasoned
2   tsp. salt
1   tsp. pepper
1   T. dried tarragon
4   tsp. honey
4   tsp. butter or margarine

Preheat oven to 350°. Slice off stem end of tomatoes and hollow out. Place open side up in a buttered baking dish. Mix bread crumbs with salt, pepper and tarragon. Drizzle honey into cavities, sprinkle with bread crumbs and top with butter. Bake uncovered for 30 minutes or until skins begin to wrinkle. Place under broiler for 2 minutes until crumbs are browned.
Note: Pretty on buffet table.

Broccoli Supreme

Serves 6 to 8

1   10-oz. package frozen
      chopped broccoli
3   carrots, sliced
1   14-oz. can artichokes
      drained, quartered
1   10½-oz. can cream of
      mushroom soup
½   cup mayonnaise
2   eggs, slightly beaten
1   tsp. lemon juice
1   tsp. Worcestershire
      sauce
1   cup shredded sharp
      Cheddar cheese
      breadcrumbs
¼   cup melted butter
      garlic salt

Cook broccoli until crisp-tender; drain and set aside. Cook carrots until tender; drain and set aside. Place artichokes in buttered 9-inch shallow casserole. Combine soup, mayonnaise, eggs, lemon juice and Worcestershire sauce; mix well. Combined soup mixture, broccoli and carrots; pour over artichokes. Sprinkle with cheese and breadcrumbs, and pour melted butter over top. Sprinkle with garlic salt. Bake for 25 minutes.

Bacon and Beans

Serves 10 to 12

12 slices bacon
 1 large onion, chopped
 ½ cup sugar
 ½ cup vinegar
 ¼ cup prepared mustard
 4 17-oz. cans green beans, undrained

Fry bacon, crumble and reserve. Saute onion in drippings; add sugar, vinegar, mustard and beans. Mix well. Cover and cook on low for 2 hours. Top with crumbled bacon.

Baked Onions

Serves 1

1 medium sweet onion
1 beef bouillon cube
1 pat of butter

Preheat oven to 350°. Peel skin from onion. Core just enough to place bullion cube in onion. Top with pat of butter. Place onion in shallow baking dish with 1-inch water. Bake about 30 minutes or until onion is cooked.
Note: Recipe may be doubled, etc.

Carrots and Apricots

Serves 4 to 6

 5 T. butter or margarine
 1 medium onion, sliced
 1 lb. carrots, shredded
 4 oz. dried apricots, cut into julienne strips
 ½ cup water
1½ tsp. Sherry wine vinegar
    salt and pepper to taste

Melt butter in skillet. Add onion and cook until golden. Add carrots and apricots. Stir-fry 2 minutes. Add water, cover, and cook until carrots are crisp-tender, 5 minutes. Uncover and cook until all liquid evaporates. Season with vinegar, salt and pepper.

C. C. Combo

Serves 6

4 cups shredded cabbage
2 carrots, shredded
⅓ cup sugar
1 T. flour
¾ tsp. dry mustard
¼ tsp. salt
2 eggs, beaten
⅛ cup vinegar
¼ cup milk

Combine cabbage and carrots; cook, covered, in boiling water for 7 minutes. Drain. Combine sugar, flour, mustard, and salt; add eggs and beat until blended. In small pan heat vinegar to boiling. Gradually stir hot vinegar into egg mixture. Return to pan. Cook, stirring constantly, until thickened and bubbly. Stir in milk; heat through. Pour over vegetables; toss lightly to blend.

Southwestern Spinach

Serves 8

2 10-oz. packages frozen
   spinach
4 T. butter
2 T. flour
2 T. chopped onion
½ cup cream or
   evaporated milk
¾ tsp. celery salt
¾ tsp. garlic salt
½ tsp. black pepper
1 cup grated Cheddar
   cheese
1 tsp. Worcestershire
   sauce
1 4-oz. can diced green
   chile
   buttered bread crumbs

Preheat oven to 350°. Cook spinach according to package directions. Drain, reserving ½ cup liquid. Saute onion in butter. Blend in flour, add milk and reserved liquid and cook until thickened. Add spinach, seasonings, cheese and chile. Pour into a 9-inch square pan, top with bread crumbs. Bake for 25 minutes.

Cheesy Green Beans

Serves 4 to 6

1 lb. green beans, cooked
¼ cup butter or margarine, melted
½ envelope dry onion soup mix
1 T. lemon juice
1 cup grated Cheddar cheese

Preheat broiler. Place beans in baking dish. Combine butter, soup mix and lemon juice; pour over beans. Top with cheese. Place under broiler until cheese melts.
Note: This quick dish also is very good with broccoli instead of green beans.

Chinese Green Beans

Serves 4

1 lb. green beans
2 T. cooking oil
½ cup water
1 tsp. salt
1 tsp. sugar

Heat oil in deep pan. Add beans and stir frequently for 5 minutes. Add water, cover and simmer 10 minutes until beans are tender. Mix in salt and sugar. Cook, uncovered 1 minute. Serve hot.

Delicious Beans

Serves 6 to 8

5 slices bacon, diced
1 small onion, chopped
½ lb. ground beef
1 lb. can butter (lima) beans, drained
1 lb. can pork and beans
⅔ lb. can kidney beans, drained
¾ cup brown sugar
½ cup ketchup
½ tsp. dry mustard
1 T. vinegar

Preheat oven to 350°. Fry bacon crisp, then saute onion. Cook ground beef. Add remaining ingredients and mix well. Put in casserole and bake for one hour.
Note: Freezes well.

Creamy Corn and Chile

Serves 8

1   8-oz. package cream
    cheese
½   cup milk
2   T. butter or margarine
2   12-oz. cans whole kernel
    corn, drained
1   4-oz. can diced green
    chile
½   tsp. garlic salt

In microwave safe container, melt cream cheese, milk and butter in microwave on ¾ power for 2 minutes or until cheese melts. Add remaining ingredients, mix well and microwave on high for 3 minutes or until hot, stirring mixture after 2 minutes.

Family Green Beans

Serves 8

2   17-oz. cans green beans,
    cooked and drained
¼   cup chopped onion
½   cup butter or margarine
1   8-oz. package cream
    cheese, softened
1   10¾-oz. can cream of
    mushroom soup
32 Ritz crackers, crushed

Preheat oven to 350°. Saute onion in butter until tender. Stir cream cheese into warm beans until melted, then add soup. With slotted spoon add onions to bean mixture. Combine crumbs with butter. Pour bean mixture into greased casserole, top with crumbs. Bake 30 minutes.

Versatile Beets

Serves 12

2   1-lb. cans beets, drained
    and sliced
½   cup plus 1 T. oil
½   cup frozen orange juice
    concentrate
½   cup cider vinegar
2   T. Dijon mustard
2   T. soy sauce
2   T. brown sugar
    salt and pepper

Heat beets. Bring oil, orange juice, vinegar, mustard, soy sauce, sugar, salt and pepper to boil in pan. Pour over beets and mix to coat. Serve warm, or refrigerate and serve chilled on lettuce.

Fancy Artichokes
Serves 8

⅔ cup mayonnaise
¼ cup butter, melted
2 T. lemon juice
½ tsp. celery salt
2 15-oz. cans artichoke
    hearts, packed in
    water, drained
¼ cup slivered almonds
¼ cup grated Parmesan
    cheese

Preheat oven to 425°. Combine mayonnaise, butter, lemon juice and celery salt in small saucepan and beat until smooth. Place over low heat, stirring constantly until heated through, do NOT boil. Place artichokes in shallow baking dish. Pour sauce over and top with almonds and cheese. Bake until heated through, about 10 minutes.

Glazed Vegetables
Serves 8 to 10

¼ cup margarine
6 to 8 medium potatoes,
    quartered
¾ lb. fresh green beans,
    cut in 2-inch pieces
4 small zucchini, cut in 1-
    inch pieces
1 cup honey

Melt margarine in foil pan. Place cut vegetables in pan and drizzle honey over. Cover pan with foil. Place on grill at low setting for 45 minutes, or until done. Keep warm in 150 degree oven until ready to serve.

Green Beans and Onions
Serves 4

1 10-oz. package frozen
    green beans, cooked
½ cup butter or margarine
4 small onions, thinly
    sliced
2 T. vinegar

Melt butter in skillet. Drain beans and add to skillet with onions. Fry onions and beans until they begin to brown. Add vinegar, stir and serve hot.

Mushroom Casserole

Serves 6 to 8

1 lb. mushrooms, sliced
2 T. flour
1 tsp. salt
1 cup whipping cream
1 2.8-oz. can French fried
  onions

Preheat oven to 350°. Place mushroom in large casserole. Sprinkle with flour and salt. Stir gently. Pour cream over mushrooms. Bake for 30 minutes. After 10 minutes when liquid bubbles, stir. After 30 minutes, top with onions and place in oven just to crisp onions. Watch carefully. They burn easily.
Note: May be made ahead and baked just before serving.

Sherry-Sauteed Mushrooms

Serves 4

2 T. butter
2 T. olive oil
¾ lb. fresh mushrooms,
  thickly sliced
½ cup chopped onion
1 cup dry Sherry wine
  salt and pepper

Melt butter with 1 T. oil in skillet. Add mushrooms and saute 2 minutes. Remove mushrooms from skillet and set aside. Reduce heat and add remaining olive oil. Add onion and cook 5 minutes until soft and golden. Stir in sherry, increase heat to high and boil 6 minutes until reduced by half. Reduce heat to low. Return mushrooms to skillet. Season with salt and pepper. Simmer 5 minutes. Serve hot.
Note: Prepare ahead and reheat before serving.

Mushrooms in Patty Shells   Serves 6

6 patty·shells, baked
1 lb. mushrooms, sliced
3 T. butter
1½ cups sour cream
¾ cup grated Parmesan
  cheese
3 T. Sherry wine

Bake patty shells according to package directions. Saute mushrooms 2 minutes in butter. Add sour cream, Parmesan, and sherry. Cook slowly until heated through. Serve in patty shells.

Mushrooms, Onions and Peas   Serves 4

2 T. butter or margarine
1 T. instant minced onion
1 4-oz. can mushrooms, drained
1 10-oz. package frozen peas
  dash pepper
  dash allspice
¼ tsp. salt

In 1-quart microwave safe casserole, combine butter and onion. Microwave covered on high for 2 minutes or until onion is tender. Add mushrooms, peas, pepper and allspice. Microwave covered on high for 5½ minutes or until peas are tender, stirring once. Season with salt.

Microwave Tomatoes   Serves 6

6 tomatoes
½ cup imitation bacon bits
¼ cup chopped celery
½ cup minced onion
½ cup bread crumbs
½ tsp. salt
2 T. butter or margarine
½ cup grated Cheddar cheese

Cut off top of tomatoes and hollow out centers. Mix pulp and all ingredients except cheese. Fill tomatoes, top with cheese. Place in microwave safe dish and microwave on high for 8 minutes, rotating dish after 4 minutes.

Only Onions
Serves 6

3 cups sliced onions
3 T. butter or margarine
¼ cup dry Sherry wine
½ tsp. sugar
½ tsp. salt
⅛ tsp. pepper
2 T. grated Parmesan
   cheese

Cook onions in butter until tender. Stir to separate rings. Add Sherry, sugar, salt and pepper. Cook 2 minutes, sprinkle with cheese and serve.

Sensational Sauerkraut
Serves 6

1 32-oz. jar sauerkraut
1 28-oz. can diced
   tomatoes
1 cup brown sugar
¼ lb. bacon, diced
1 small onion, diced

Preheat oven to 350°. Mix all ingredients and bake uncovered for 3 hours. Stir occasionally. Add water if too dry.

Note: Keeps well in the refrigerator for a week.

Variations: Add sausage, hot dogs, etc. to casserole during last 30 minutes.

Chinese Celery
Serves 5

2 T. butter or margarine
2 T. slivered almonds
4 medium stalks celery,
   sliced
1 medium onion, sliced
2 T. soy sauce
1 8-oz. can sliced water
   chestnuts, drained
1 4-oz. can mushrooms,
   drained

Combine all ingredients in skillet. Simmer covered, 15 minutes or until celery is cooked, stirring occasionally.

Sesame Green Beans
Serves 6

1 lb. green beans, cut
   julienne
3 T. soy sauce
1 T. sesame oil
¼ tsp. nutmeg
4 large mushrooms, sliced
½ cup sesame seeds,
   toasted

Cook beans until crisp-tender, about 10 minutes. Combine soy sauce, oil and nutmeg in large skillet over medium heat. Add mushrooms and saute until just tender. Add beans and sesame seeds and toss lightly.

Spinach Souffle
Serves 4 to 6

1 12-oz. package frozen
   spinach souffle,
   thawed
2 eggs
3 T. milk
2 tsp. onion, chopped
½ cup sliced mushrooms,
   fresh or canned-
   drained
¾ cup cooked crumbled
   sausage, drained
1 cup Mozzarella cheese

Preheat oven to 400°. Grease a 9-inch pie plate. Combine all ingredients. Pour into pie plate and bake for 25 to 35 minutes.
Note: Serve for brunch with fruit and rolls.

Southwest Vegetable Casserole
Serves 12

2 cups cooked rice
1 10¾-oz. can cream of
   mushroom soup
1 cup grated Cheddar
   cheese
4 cups mixed vegetables,
   cooked
1 4-oz. can diced green
   chile

Preheat oven to 350°. Lightly grease 13 x 9 x 2-inch pan. Mix all ingredients, place in pan and bake, uncovered for 30 to 45 minutes or until hot and bubbly.
Note: Freezes well.

Stuffed Vegetables

Serves 8

4   bell peppers
4   tomatoes
1½ lb. ground beef
3   large onions, chopped
3   cups cooked rice
2   tsp. tarragon
½   tsp. mint
½   tsp. turmeric
1   bunch of parsley,
     minced
1   cup tomato sauce,
     divided
    salt to taste
2½ cups water
3   T. lemon juice

Clean vegetables inside and out, keeping them intact for stuffing. Cook beef, add onions and cook until golden. Combine beef, onions, rice, tarragon, mint, turmeric, parsley, tomato sauce (reserving 2 T.) and salt to taste. If mixture is dry, add a little water. Fill the vegetables with the mixture, cover, and cook in water, 2 T. tomato sauce and lemon juice for 30 minutes or until done.

Variation: Eggplant, zucchini, cabbage leaves etc. may also be stuffed.

Swiss Baked Onions

Serves 6 to 8

½   cup butter
6   medium onions, sliced
1   10¾-oz. can cream of
     mushroom soup
1   cup milk
    salt and pepper
¾   lb. Swiss cheese, grated
    French bread, sliced
    melted butter

Preheat oven to 350°. Butter 2 quart shallow baking dish. Melt ½ cup butter in large skillet. Add onions and cook until translucent, stirring frequently, 15 minutes. Transfer onions to dish. Combine soup, milk, salt and pepper in bowl. Pour over onions. Sprinkle with grated cheese. Dip bread slices in melted butter on one side. Arrange buttered side up over onion mixture to cover completely. Bake until bread is browned, 30 minutes.

Microwave Butternut Squash   Serves 4 to 6

6 T. margarine
2 cups cooked, peeled, mashed squash
½ cup sugar
2 eggs
1 cup milk
½ tsp. nutmeg
½ tsp. cinnamon
¾ cup corn flakes
½ cup nuts
¼ cup brown sugar
6 T. butter

Melt margarine in microwave safe casserole. Add squash, sugar, eggs, milk, nutmeg and cinnamon, stir well. Cover with wax paper and cook on high for 10 to 12 minutes, turning casserole 3 times. Combine corn flakes, nuts, brown sugar and butter. Remove casserole from microwave and top with corn flake mixture. Cover with waxed paper and cook on high for 2 minutes.

Stove Squash   Serves 6

1 lb. yellow squash
½ cup butter
1 4-oz. can diced green chile
¾ cup chopped onion
1 cup grated Cheddar cheese
1 cup sliced water chestnuts
½ cup mayonnaise
1 tsp. sugar
1 egg, beaten
salt and pepper to taste

Slice squash and cook slowly in saucepan with butter 10 minutes. Add remaining ingredients and cook another 5 minutes until vegetables are tender and heated through.

Rice Broccoli Casserole

Serves 6 to 8

2 cups cooked rice
3 cups diced, cooked
   chicken
20 oz. chopped broccoli,
   cooked
2 T. margarine
2 large onions, chopped
6 stalks celery chopped
2 10¾-oz. cans cream of
   mushroom soup
2 10¾-oz. cans cream of
   chicken soup
1 16-oz. jar Cheese Whiz

Preheat oven to 350°. Lightly grease shallow baking dish. Mix rice, chicken and broccoli, and place in baking dish. Melt margarine and saute onions and celery. Add soups and cheese. Simmer 5 minutes, stirring constantly so it doesn't burn. Pour sauce mixture over chicken mixture. Bake for 30 minutes.

Note: Good family supper.

Topped Cauliflower

Serves 8

1 large head cauliflower
½ cup olive oil
3 cloves garlic, minced
2 T. snipped parsley
1 T. sesame seeds, toasted
   salt and pepper to taste

Cook cauliflower florets in boiling water until tender. Cook garlic and parsley in oil until crisp. Drain cauliflower; top with garlic mixture and sesame seeds.

Note: Topping goes well on broccoli as well.

Topped Tomatoes

Serves 4

2 T. imitation bacon bits
½ cup sour cream
½ tsp. seasoned salt
4 medium tomatoes

Blend bacon bits, sour cream and salt. Cut ends off tomatoes, and cut tomatoes in half. Place tomatoes in microwave safe dish. Top each half with sour cream mixture. Microwave on high for 4 minutes or until tomatoes are heated through.

Homemade Egg Noodles   Serves 12 to 15

6 cups flour
7 eggs
6 T. oil
3 drops yellow food
    coloring
¼ tsp. butter flavoring

Place flour in bowl. Add remaining ingredients. (All liquids together measure just under 2¼ cups. If short, add water.) Knead until well combined. Cover and let dough rest for 1 hour. Roll out and cut as desired.

Note: Recipe can be halved. Fresh pasta cooks very quickly. Boil 1 minute and check if it is done. Store dry pasta covered, at room temperature.

Luscious Linguini   Serves 4

¼ cup olive oil
¼ cup butter
1 T. flour
1 cup chicken broth
1 clove garlic
2 tsp. dried parsley
2 tsp. lemon juice
   salt and pepper to taste
1 14-oz. can artichoke
    hearts, drained and
    quartered
4 T. grated Parmesan
    cheese, divided
2 tsp. drained capers
1 T. butter
1 T. olive oil
1 lb. linguini, cooked and
    drained

Heat oil and butter. Add flour and stir until smooth. Add broth stirring until thickened. Add garlic, parsley, lemon juice, salt and pepper and cook 5 minutes stirring constantly. Add artichokes, 3 T. cheese and capers. Cover and simmer 10 minutes. Heat remaining butter and oil. Add pasta and 1 T. cheese. Toss to coat. Pour sauce over pasta. Serve topped with proscuitto and additional Parmesan cheese.

Note: A pasta lover's dream!

Noodles Romanoff

Serves 6 to 8

1 lb. package egg noodles,
    cooked and drained
⅓ cup chopped onion
1 16-oz. container cottage
    cheese
1 16-oz. container sour
    cream
1 tsp. Worcestershire
    sauce
1 tsp. salt
¼ tsp. garlic powder
⅛ tsp. pepper
4 slices American cheese
    cut in half diagonally

Preheat oven to 350°. Grease a 2½ quart shallow baking dish. In large bowl combine all ingredients except American cheese; mix well. Turn into baking dish. Cover and bake 25 to 30 minutes. Uncover; top with American cheese and bake 5 minutes longer.

Pasta Primavera

Serves 4

8 oz. spaghetti, cooked
1½ tsp. salt
1 10-oz. package frozen
    peas
½ cup sliced celery
1 carrot, cut in julienne
    strips
1½ cups broccoli florets
2 T. olive oil
1½ tsp. minced garlic
1½ tsp. dried basil
¼ cup chopped parsley
5 T. butter
1 cup whipping cream
½ cup grated Parmesan
    cheese

Cook spaghetti according to package directions. Bring 4 cups water to boil in pot. Add salt, peas, celery and carrot. Cook 2 minutes. Stir in broccoli; cook 3 minutes. Drain. Heat oil, stir in garlic, basil and parsley. Cook 2 minutes. Remove from heat and mix in vegetables. Drain spaghetti. Melt butter, add cream and cheese. Stir 2 minutes, until cheese is melted. Add spaghetti and toss to coat with sauce. Add half the vegetables; toss to mix. Pile onto plates and top with remaining vegetables.

Cottage Cheese Squares   Serves 8

2 lbs. dry cottage cheese
4 eggs
1 T. sour cream
1 tsp. salt
½ cup flour

Combine cheese, eggs, sour cream and salt. Gradually add just enough flour to make a stiff dough. Knead until well blended. Roll to ⅛-inch thickness on floured board. Cut and place in rapidly boiling water. Boil 8 minutes. Serve topped with melted butter.

Instant Pasta   Serves 4

2 3-oz. packages Dry
   Ramen Noodle Soup
¼ lb. butter

Cook pasta for one minute in boiling water. Drain. Melt butter in skillet. Add pasta and seasonings. Stir fry to coat pasta.
Variations: Vegetables may be added for a Pasta Primavera. Meat may also be added for an entire meal in one pan.

Italian Noodle Casserole   Serves 4

1 8-oz. package flat egg
   noodles, cooked and
   drained
3 tsp. Italian seasoning
1 pint sour cream
¼ cup grated Parmesan
   cheese

Combine seasoning and sour cream. Heat to boiling, but do NOT boil. Add Parmesan to sauce. Fold in noodles and serve.
Note: Quick, easy and very good. Serve with Scallopini, salad and garlic bread.

Kugel

Serves 8 to 12

1 1-lb. carton cottage cheese
4 oz. cream cheese, room temperature
½ cup butter, room temperature
1 cup milk
4 eggs
¼ cup sugar
½ tsp. salt
3 cups noodles, freshly cooked
1 tsp. vanilla

Butter 9 x 13-inch baking dish. Blend cottage cheese, cream cheese and butter in large bowl. Mix in milk, eggs, sugar and salt. Fold in noodles and vanilla. Transfer to prepared dish. (Can be prepared a day ahead; cover and refrigerate.) Preheat oven to 325°. Bake kugel until lightly browned and edges begin to pull away from sides, about 50 minutes. Cut into squares. Serve kugel warm.

Popover Pizza

Serves 6

12 oz. pepperoni
½ cup chopped onion
1 T. butter or margarine
1 15½-oz. jar spaghetti sauce
½ tsp. fennel seed
12 oz. sliced Mozzarella cheese
2 eggs
1 cup milk
1 T. cooking oil
1 cup flour
½ tsp. salt
¼ cup Parmesan cheese

Preheat oven to 400°. In skillet cook pepperoni and onion in butter until onion is tender. Drain. Stir in spaghetti sauce and fennel. Pour mixture into ungreased 13 x 9 x 2-inch baking pan. Arrange sliced mozzarella on top. Combine eggs, milk and oil in bowl; add flour and salt. Beat with rotary beater until smooth. Pour batter over cheese. Top with Parmesan. Bake for 30 minutes or until crust is golden. Cut into squares. Serve hot.

Creamy Fettuccine
Serves 4

8 thick-cut bacon slices, chopped
8 green onions, chopped
1 cup whipping cream
1 cup Parmesan cheese
⅔ cup chopped fresh basil, or 3 T. dried basil
1 lb. fettuccine, cooked
   salt and pepper

Cook bacon until it is beginning to brown. Add onions and stir 1 minute to soften. Add cream and simmer 1 minute until it begins to thicken. Mix in cheese and basil. Add sauce to hot pasta and stir to coat. Season with salt and pepper. Serve immediately, passing additional cheese.
Note: Recipe can be halved.

Pasta with Pesto Sauce
Serves 4

2 cups (firmly packed) fresh basil leaves
¾ cup Parmesan cheese
¼ cup pine nuts
4 cloves garlic
½ cup olive oil
1 lb. pasta, cooked

Combine basil, cheese, pine nuts and garlic in blender and puree. With machine running, gradually add oil until mixture is consistency of thick mayonnaise. Combine pasta and sauce, toss well. Serve.

Pronto Pasta
Serves 4 to 6

8 oz. pasta, cooked
1 4-oz. can diced green chile
1 cup sour cream
1 cup cottage cheese
¼ tsp. garlic salt
   Parmesan cheese

While pasta is cooking, combine chile, sour cream, cottage cheese, and garlic salt. Heat in microwave until hot. Pour over cooked pasta and top with grated Parmesan cheese. Serve.

Linguine with Nuts and Ham   Serves 4

⅓ cup olive oil
½ lb. cooked ham, chopped
½ cup chopped walnuts
2 T. minced parsley
1 clove garlic, minced
1 lb. linguine, cooked
grated Parmesan cheese

Heat oil in large skillet over medium heat. Add ham, nuts, parsley and garlic; saute 4 minutes. Add linguine and toss until heated through. Serve with Parmesan cheese.

Pasta Inverno   Serves 4

8 oz. noodles
2 cups cooked and diced meat, fish or poultry
½ tsp. oregano flakes
4 T. oil or butter
2 cloves garlic, minced
¾ cup cream or milk
1 egg
salt and pepper
½ cup grated Parmesan cheese
¼ cup chopped parsley

Cook noodles according to package instructions. Sprinkle meat with oregano; set aside. Heat oil in skillet and saute garlic. Beat cream with egg, salt and pepper; add to skillet, stirring. Bring to a simmer, add meat and Parmesan cheese. Heat through, stirring. Pour over drained noodles, top with parsley.

Seasoned Spinach Noodles   Serves 4

½ lb. spinach noodles
¼ cup butter
1 clove garlic, minced
¼ cup grated Parmesan cheese
¼ cup grated Swiss or Gruyere cheese

Cook noodles according to package directions. In skillet heat butter and saute garlic 1 minute. Drain pasta, pour butter over and toss to coat. Top with cheeses and toss again. Serve.

Pasta Squares

Serves 6

8 oz. medium noodles,
    cooked and drained
2 eggs, beaten
1¼ cups milk
½ tsp. salt
⅛ tsp. pepper
1 8-oz. can pizza sauce
¾ cup shredded
    Mozzarella cheese
¾ cup shredded Provolone
    cheese

Preheat oven to 400°. Combine eggs, milk, salt and pepper. Stir in noodles. Pour noodle mixture into buttered 8-inch square baking pan. Bake 15 minutes, or until set. Spread pizza sauce over noodle mixture. Sprinkle with cheeses. Bake 10 additional minutes. Cut into squares and serve.

Fettuccine with New Mexico Pecans

Serves 4

3 T. butter or margarine
¼ cup diced onion
3 T. diced red bell pepper
2 tsp. minced garlic
1 cup whipping cream
½ cup chopped pecans
¼ lb. smoked chicken, cut
    in julienne strips
¼ cup ricotta cheese,
    drained if necessary
2 T. minced fresh cilantro
10 oz. fettuccine, cooked
    and drained
    salt and pepper

Melt butter in heavy large skillet. Add onion, bell pepper and garlic and saute until softened, about 5 minutes. Add cream, pecans, chicken, cheese and cilantro and bring to boil, stirring constantly. Set sauce aside. Add fettuccine to sauce. Cook over medium heat until heated through, stirring occasionally. Season with salt and pepper. Divide pasta among plates and serve.
Variation: Smoked turkey may be substituted for the chicken.

Pasta with Cream Sauce   Serves 4

3 cups whipping cream
⅛ tsp. nutmeg
4 cups hot cooked pasta
1 cup Parmesan cheese
2 T. butter or margarine

In a 12-inch frying pan over high heat, stir whipping cream and nutmeg until big, shiny bubbles form all over and sauce is reduced by about ⅓. Add pasta and gently mix in Parmesan and butter.

Pasta with Labor Day Sauce   Serves 6 to 8

½ lb. butter
¼ cup tomato paste
½ cup whipping cream
¼ tsp. rubbed sage
1½ tsp. Hungarian paprika
2 - 4 cloves garlic, minced
¾ cup Parmesan cheese
1 lb. pasta, cooked

Melt butter and whisk in tomato paste and cream. Add sage, paprika and garlic. Simmer 3 minutes. Whisk in the Parmesan cheese. Pour over pasta and pass additional cheese and a pepper mill. *Note: Fast, easy and delicious.*

Fabulous Fettuccine   Serves 6

2 cups sour cream
³ cup grated Parmeson cheese
¼ cup dry Vermouth
1 T. flour
1 lemon juice
2 garlic cloves, minced
½ tsp. oregano, crushed
½ tsp. basil, crushed
½ tsp. marjoram, crushed
   salt and pepper to taste
½ cup butter, melted
1 lb. fettuccine, cooked and drained

Combine first 10 ingredients in pan and simmer for 20 minutes. Combine with fettuccine and toss to coat. Serve immediately.

Country Style New Potatoes   Serves 8

2½ to 3 lb. new potatoes
½ cup butter
3 T. flour
1 tsp. salt
¼ tsp. pepper
2 cups water
6 slices bacon
1 T. lemon juice
  snipped fresh dill and
    parsley

Cook potatoes in skins. Melt butter, stir in flour, salt and pepper. Slowly add water and stir until thickened. Add lemon juice. Heat oven to 325°. Saute bacon until crisp. When potatoes are tender, remove band of skin around center of each. Put in casserole. Pour sauce over potatoes. Bake 20 minutes. Top with bacon, dill and parsley.

Creamed Chile Potatoes   Serves 6

2½ lb. potatoes, cooked,
    peeled, cubed or
    sliced
4 T. butter
4 T. flour
2 cups milk
1 tsp. salt
¼ tsp. pepper
2 cloves garlic, minced
1 4-oz. can diced green
    chile
2 cups shredded Cheddar
    cheese
  buttered bread crumbs

Preheat oven to 350°. Grease 1½ quart baking dish. Place potatoes in dish. Melt butter, add garlic and saute until transparent. Remove from heat; blend in flour. Return to heat; stir and cook until mixture is bubbly. Remove from heat; add liquid. Mix well. Add salt, pepper and cheese. Stir until cheese melts. Add chile. Pour sauce over potatoes and mix to coat. Top with crumbs and paprika. Bake 20 minutes or until heated through.

Fluffy Sweet Potatoes

Serves 6 to 8

3 eggs, separated
3 cups mashed sweet
   potatoes
4 T. brown sugar
½ cup butter, melted
1 tsp. vanilla
2 T. wine, rum or brandy
½ tsp. cinnamon
½ tsp. nutmeg
   salt and pepper to taste

Preheat oven to 350°. Grease a 1-quart casserole. Beat egg yolks well. Add rest of ingredients except egg whites. Beat whites to stiff peaks and fold into yolk mixture. Bake 20 to 25 minutes.

Leftover Potatoes

Serves 6 to 8

¼ cup butter or margarine
¼ cup oil
7 large potatoes, cooked,
   peeled and sliced
   into ½-inch thick
   rounds
4 green onions, minced
   salt and pepper to taste
1 cup sour cream

Heat butter and oil in skillet. Add potatoes and cook until golden, turning once. Add onions and cook 2 minutes. Season with salt and pepper. Place potatoes on serving platter and top with dollops of sour cream.
Note: This is a good way to use leftover cooked potatoes.

Ranch Potatoes

Serves 4 to 6

2 lb. small red new
   potatoes, cooked
½ cup sliced green onions
1 cup prepared Hidden
   Valley Ranch
   Dressing

Cube or slice potatoes while warm. Gently toss potatoes, onions and dressing. Serve warm.
Note: Any leftovers can be served as potato salad the next day.

Quick Crisp Potatoes   Serves 4

4 medium potatoes,
   peeled and patted
   dry
⅛ tsp. garlic salt
⅛ tsp. garlic powder
⅛ tsp. paprika
½ cup dehydrated onion
   flakes
4 T. oil
   parsley flakes

Slice potatoes thinly and evenly. Arrange half of slices in microwave safe dish. Sprinkle with garlic salt, garlic powder and paprika. Top with ¼ cup onion flakes. Repeat layer. Pour oil over top. Cover and microwave on high until potatoes are fork tender, about 15 minutes. Sprinkle with parsley flakes.

Skillet-Baked Potatoes with Rosemary
                                        Serves 8

4 lb. red new potatoes,
   cooked, peeled and
   quartered
⅔ cup olive oil
4 T. chopped fresh
   rosemary or 2 tsp.
   dried, crumbled
1½ tsp. coarse salt
   pepper to taste
2 T. butter, cut into small
   pieces

Divide potatoes between 2 skillets. Drizzle ⅓ cup oil into each. Sprinkle 2 T. rosemary and ¾ tsp. salt into each. Season with pepper. Toss potatoes to coat. Dot each with 1 T. butter. Cover and cook 20 minutes, shaking skillets and turning potatoes occasionally until brown on all sides. Serve immediately.
Note: Crisp and crunchy on the outside, tender inside - an irresistible combination.

Lithuanian Kugelis   Serves 6

5 medium potatoes,
   peeled and cubed
3 eggs
1 large onion, chopped
¼ tsp. pepper
1½ tsp. salt
¼ cup butter or bacon fat
⅓ cup flour
¼ cup milk

Preheat oven to 350°. Grease deep 2-quart casserole. Mix all ingredients in blender until potatoes are chopped. Bake uncovered, 1 hour or until browned and set in center. Serve hot with sour cream.

Potatoes Deluxe   Serves 4

1 clove garlic, minced
1 onion, sliced
3 T. butter or margarine
2 large potatoes, peeled
   and sliced
¾ cup whipping cream
½ cup milk
1 tsp. salt
⅛ tsp. pepper
⅛ tsp. nutmeg

Cook garlic and onion in butter for 5 minutes until tender. Add potatoes, cream, milk, salt, pepper and nutmeg. Cover and cook over low heat for 25 minutes or until potatoes are tender. Stir occasionally. Serve hot.
Note: Recipe may be doubled or tripled.

Potato Pancakes   Serves 8

8 potatoes, peeled and
   grated
½ onion, minced
3 eggs, beaten
1 tsp. salt
1 T. flour
   butter, bacon fat, or oil

Combine all ingredients except butter. Fry pancakes in skillet until golden. Serve hot with sour cream.

Cantonese Fried Rice   Serves 8

3   eggs
2   tsp. salt
½   tsp. dry sherry
2   T. onion, minced
5   T. cooking oil
4   cups cooked rice
½   tsp. browning sauce
1   cup bean sprouts

Beat eggs with salt and sherry. Heat oil in skillet and stir in onion for 30 seconds. Add egg mixture, scramble and break into small pieces until dry. Add rice, browning sauce, and bean sprouts. Stir fry for 8 minutes until all ingredients are well blended and heated through.
Variation: 1 cup diced cooked meat may be added to rice.

Lemon Rice   Serves 4 to 6

1   cup chopped onion
1   clove garlic, minced
2   T. butter or margarine
1   cup rice
1   14-oz. can chicken broth
¼   tsp. white pepper
2   egg yolks
2   T. lemon juice
    pinch nutmeg

Saute onion and garlic in butter until soft. Add rice and cook for 1 minute. Add chicken broth and pepper. Bring to a boil. Reduce heat, cover, and cook 20 minutes, until all liquid is absorbed. Remove from heat and let stand, covered, for 5 minutes. Beat yolks, lemon juice and nutmeg. Gradually stir into hot, cooked rice, mixing well. Cover, let stand 3 minutes.

Brown Rice   Serves 8

2   cups brown rice, cooked
2   eggs
⅓   cup crisp bacon,
       crumbled

Mix all ingredients in pan and heat thoroughly for about 5 minutes. Top with parsley.

Rice Pilaf   Serves 12

2 cups white rice
1 cup wild rice
1 T. dehydrated instant,
     minced onions
2 tsp. chicken bouillon
1 T. butter or margarine
1 T. parsley
6 cups water

Combine all ingredients and cook in microwave on medium-low for about 20 minutes. Let stand 5 minutes before serving.

Variation: A can of drained sliced mushrooms is a nice addition to this.

Do-Ahead Eggs Mornay   Serves 6

6 slices bread, crusts
     trimmed, cubed
4 eggs
2 cups milk
½ lb. grated cheese
½ tsp. dry mustard
⅛ tsp. pepper
2 4-oz. cans diced green
     chile

Grease 9 x 13-inch baking dish. Put bread in pan. Top with cheese then chile. Beat eggs, milk, mustard and pepper. Pour over bread. Cover and refrigerate overnight. Bake 35 minutes at 350°.

Note: Handy dish when you have overnight guests.

Home-Style Pork and Beans   Serves 6 to 8

1 31-oz. can pork and
     beans in tomato
     sauce
½ cup packed brown sugar
¼ cup ketchup
1 T. instant minced onion
½ tsp. Worcestershire
     sauce

Heat all ingredients. Simmer, uncovered, for 10 minutes, stirring occasionally.

Blintz Souffle

Serves 4

1 lb. cottage cheese
3 oz. cream cheese, room
    temperature
¼ cup butter, melted
6 T. sugar
½ cup flour
3 eggs
½ tsp. fresh lemon juice
½ tsp. baking powder
½ tsp. cinnamon
    sour cream

Heat oven to 350°. Grease 8 inch baking pan with 2-inch high sides. Combine cottage cheese, butter and sugar in medium bowl. Add flour, eggs, lemon juice and baking powder and stir well. Spoon batter into prepared pan. Sprinkle with cinnamon. Bake until edges are light brown and souffle is springy to touch, about 45 minutes. Serve, passing sour cream separately.

Note: This outstanding dish has never been easier. Try it, you'll like it!

Southwest Egg and Sausage Dish

Serves 10 to 12

1 lb. bulk sausage, cooked
    (medium hot)
½ lb. fresh mushrooms,
    sauteed
1 4-oz. can green chile
5 eggs, beaten
6 slices bread, cubed
2 cups milk
1 tsp. dry mustard
1 tsp. salt
⅛ tsp. Worcestershire
    sauce
1 cup grated cheese

Grease 9 x 13 inch baking dish. Beat eggs; add bread, mushrooms, milk, mustard, salt, Worcestershire sauce, cheese and sausage. Mix well. Put in pan, cover and refrigerate overnight. Preheat oven to 350°. Bake casserole covered for 45 minutes. Reduce heat to 325°; uncover and bake an additional 15 minutes.

Note: Sunday would be simplified with this easy, make ahead breakfast or brunch.

Santa Fe Omelet

Serves 4

4 T. margarine, divided
½ cup chopped green chile
¼ cup sliced green onion
6 eggs
½ tsp. salt
⅓ cup mayonnaise
1 cup cooked noodles
1 cup grated Cheddar cheese, divided

In 8 inch omelet pan melt 1 T. margarine. Saute vegetables; remove. Beat eggs, salt and mayonnaise, stir in vegetables and noodles. Pour ¾ cup of mixture into pan covering the bottom. Top with ¼ cup of cheese. Cook about 5 minutes or until firm. Fold in half. Repeat 3 times. Serve hot with taco sauce if desired.

Mexican Chile Pie

Serves 6 to 8

1 baked 9 inch pie shell
1½ cup crushed cheese flavored tortilla chips
1 15-oz. can beans with Mexican seasoning
1 4-oz. can diced green chile, drained
½ cup sliced, pitted ripe olives
¼ cup sliced green onions
½ cup sour cream
½ cup shredded Monterey Jack cheese
½ cup shredded Cheddar cheese
1 2½-oz. jar sliced mushrooms
    sliced ripe olives

Preheat oven to 375°. Sprinkle 1 cup of chips in crust. Combine beans, diced chile, olives and onions. Spread over chips in crust. Dot with sour cream. Top with mushrooms and olives, then cheeses and finally chips. Cover lightly with foil. Bake for 15 minutes. Uncover and bake 20 minutes longer. Garnish with tomatoes and avocados if desired.

Brunch Bake   Serves 6

2   T. butter
10 eggs, beaten
½   cup sour cream
8   slices salami, chopped
½   cup onion, chopped
1   cup Chedder cheese,
       grated
12 cherry tomatoes, halved
1   4-oz. can mushrooms,
       drained
    salt and pepper to taste

Preheat oven to 350°. Melt butter in 2-quart baking dish. combine remaining ingredients and pour into prepared dish. Bake 30 minutes or until golden. Serve immediately.

Cheese Crusted Quiche   Serves 4

1   lb. sliced Muenster
       cheese
6   eggs, beaten
½   cup whole milk
1   4-oz. can diced green
       chile
¼   tsp. Tobasco
    salt and pepper to taste

Preheat oven to 375°. Line bottom and sides of 4 ramekins with cheese slices. Combine remaining ingredients and divide among ramekins. Bake for 20 minutes. Let stand 5 minutes before serving.

South-of-the-Border Eggs   Serves 4

2   cups taco sauce
8   eggs, fried
4   flour tortillas

Heat sauce. Place eggs on tortillas and top with sauce.

Desserts

SHIPROCK

A majestic rock formation in Northwestern New Mexico, Shiprock is called by the Navajos *TSE BIDA' HI*, meaning *Rock with Wings*. A Navajo legend tells of the People cast up from the earth at this spot, and the ship is a symbol of their voyage.

Blueberry Cheese Treats

Yields 6 dozen

1½ cups vanilla wafer
    crumbs
½ cup powdered sugar
½ cup butter, melted
1 cup sugar
1 8-oz. package cream
    cheese, softened
2 eggs, beaten
2½ T. lemon juice
1 21-oz. can blueberry pie
    filling

Preheat oven to 350°. Grease 9 x 13-inch pan or mini muffin tins. Mix crumbs, powdered sugar and butter. Press mixture into bottom of pan. Mix sugar, cheese and eggs until smooth. Spread over wafer mixture. Bake for 20 minutes. Cool thoroughly. Stir lemon juice into pie filling. Spread over cheese mixture. Cover and refrigerate. Cut and serve.

Brownies Deluxe

Yields 4 dozen

1 cup butter
4 1-oz. squares chocolate
½ tsp. salt
2 cups sugar
4 whole eggs
1½ cups flour
¾ cup sour cream
1 cup chopped nuts

Preheat oven to 350°. Grease 11 x 15-inch pan. Melt butter and chocolate, mix in salt and sugar. Add eggs, beating well after each addition. Add flour and mix. Stir in sour cream and nuts. Bake for 30 minutes.

Fruit 'N Nut Cups

Yields 5 dozen

1 7-oz. can coconut
2 cups pecans
1 lb. chopped dates
1 can sweetened
    condensed milk
30 Maraschino cherries,
    halved

Preheat oven to 250°. Grease miniature muffin cups. Mix all ingredients except cherries. Fill muffin cups with batter, top with cherry half. Bake for 35 minutes.
Note: Freezes well. A cup of chocolate chips may be added.

Cherry Petites

Yields 4 dozen

2 cups flour
¾ cup butter or margarine
¾ cup sugar
½ tsp. salt
1 8-oz. package cream cheese, softened
⅓ cup sugar
1 egg
¼ cup cut Maraschino cherries
¼ cup almonds, sliced
½ cup chocolate chips

Preheat oven to 375°. Combine flour, butter, ¾ cup sugar and salt. Beat on low speed of mixer until particles are fine. Press ⅔ of mixture firmly into bottom of 9 x 13-inch pan. Bake for 15 minutes. Blend cream cheese, ⅓ cup sugar and egg until smooth. Stir in remaining ingredients. Spread on crust. Sprinkle with remaining crumbs. Bake 25 minutes or until golden.

Chocolate Zucchini Bars

Yields 5 dozen

BARS:
4 eggs
2 cups sugar
1½ cups oil
2 tsp. baking soda
2 cups flour
2 tsp. cinnamon
¼ cup cocoa
1 tsp. vanilla
3 cups grated zucchini
1 cup nuts
FROSTING:
3 T. milk
6 T. butter or margarine
1½ cups sugar
½ cup chocolate chips

Preheat oven to 350°. Grease 11 x 15-inch pan. Beat eggs, sugar and oil for 2 minutes. Add dry ingredients and mix well. Stir in vanilla, zucchini and nuts. Pour into pan and bake for 30 minutes or until done. Cool. To make frosting bring milk, butter and sugar to a boil. Boil for 30 seconds. Remove from heat and add chips. Stir until smooth. Spread on warm bars.

Cookies a la Casa   **Yields 8 dozen**

- 2 **cups butter**
- 2 **cups sugar**
- 2 **cups (packed) brown sugar**
- 4 **eggs**
- 2 **tsp. vanilla**
- 4 **cups flour**
- 5 **cups oatmeal**
- 2 **tsp. baking powder**
- 2 **tsp. baking soda**
- 1 **30-oz.bag of chocolate chips**
- 1 **cup chopped nuts**
- 1 **cup Grape-nuts**
- 1 **cup All-Bran**
- 1 **cup chopped dates**
- 2 **cups raisins**

Preheat oven to 375°. Cream together butter and sugars. Add eggs and vanilla. Add flour, oatmeal, baking powder and soda. Mix well. Add chips, nuts, Grape-nuts, All-Bran, dates and raisins. Place ⅛ to ¼ cup of batter 2 inches apart on ungreased cookie sheet. Bake 6 minutes. Allow to cool completely on cookie sheet before removing.
Note: Freezes well. This after school favorite for kids of all ages is tasty and nutritious.

Deluxe Lemon Bars   **Yields 48 bars**

- 2¼ **cups flour, divided**
- ½ **cup powdered sugar**
- 1 **cup butter, room temperature**
- 4 **eggs, beaten**
- 2 **cups sugar**
- ½ **cup lemon juice**
- ½ **tsp. baking powder**
  powdered sugar

Preheat oven to 350°. Lightly grease 13 x 9-inch baking pan. Sift 2 cups flour and powdered sugar. Cut in butter until mixture clings together. Press into pan. Bake for 20 minutes or until lightly tan. Remove from oven. Beat eggs, adding sugar slowly, then lemon juice. Sift together ¼ cup flour with baking powder. Stir into egg mixture. Pour over baked crust. Bake for another 25 minutes. When cool, top with additional powdered sugar.
Note: Freezes well.

Date Bars

Yields 4 dozen

3 eggs
1 cup sugar
1 cup flour
1 tsp. baking powder
1½ cups pitted, chopped
    dates
1 cup chopped pecans
1 tsp. vanilla
  powdered sugar

Preheat oven to 350°. Line 9 x 13 inch pan with waxed paper. Beat eggs and sugar until thick. Add sifted dry ingredients and beat until smooth. Add dates, vanilla and nuts. Put in pan and bake 30 minutes. Cut into strips while warm and roll in powdered sugar.
Note: Freezes well.

Microwave Persian Squares

Yields 6 dozen

2 cups graham cracker
    crumbs
2 cups flaked coconut
1 cup chopped pecans
½ cup sugar
½ cups cocoa
2¾ cups margarine, divided
2 eggs
6 T. dry instant vanilla
    pudding mix
4 cups powdered sugar
¼ cup milk
4 cups chocolate chips

In bowl mix crumbs, coconut and pecans. In microwave cook on high ½ cup sugar, cocoa, 1 cup margarine, and eggs until thick. Add to above crumb mixture. Mix and press into 13 x 16 x 1-inch pan. Place in freezer while preparing next layer. Melt 1 cup margarine in microwave, add pudding, powdered sugar and milk. Spread over first layer. Return to freezer while making the last layer. In microwave melt chocolate chips and ¾ cup margarine. Mix and top Persian Squares. Refrigerate until set.
Note: Refrigerate or freeze.

Coconut Meringue Drops

Yields 8 dozen

2 egg whites, room
    temperature
4 T. sugar
5 T. powdered sugar
1 T. flour
¼ tsp. vanilla
1 cup shredded coconut

Preheat oven to 350°. Line cookie sheet with brown paper. Beat egg whites until foamy. Add dry ingredients 2 T. at a time. Beat until stiff. Fold in vanilla and coconut. Drop from tsp. onto cookie sheet. Bake for 20 minutes or until golden brown.

Note: This cookie is extremely inexpensive.

Old Fashioned Oatmeal Cookies

Yields 5 dozen

1 cup raisins
1 cup water
1 cup sugar
¾ cup butter or margarine
2 eggs
1 tsp. vanilla
2 cups oats, regular or
    quick
2½ cups flour
1 tsp. baking soda
½ tsp. baking powder
1 tsp. salt
1 tsp. cinnamon
½ tsp. cloves
¼ tsp. nutmeg

Cook raisins in water for 10 minutes. Drain and reserve liquid. Cream sugar and butter, add eggs, and vanilla. Blend in drained raisins. Add water to reserved liquid to make ½ cup. Add to batter. Blend in oats, flour, soda, powder, salt, cinnamon, cloves and nutmeg. Mix well. Drop by tsp. on lightly greased cookie sheet. Press lightly with floured glass. Bake 6 minutes or until done.

Note: These are also good with nuts. Dates can be substituted for raisins. You can also use whole wheat flour, or half wheat and half white flour.

Oatmeal Bars

Yields 4 dozen

1 cup raisins
¾ cup water
1 cup rolled oats
1 cup flour
⅓ cup shortening
½ cup sugar
1 egg
1 tsp. salt
1 tsp. cinnamon
1 tsp. vanilla
¾ tsp. baking soda
¼ tsp. nutmeg
½ cup chopped nuts

Preheat oven to 350°. Grease 9 x 13-inch pan. Combine raisins with water; simmer 10 minutes. Combine oats with raisins and liquid. Add remaining ingredients. Blend, then beat at medium speed for 1 minute. Spread evenly in pan. Bake for 20 minutes or until top springs back when touched.

Note: For high altitude (5000 feet), decrease soda to ½ tsp. and bake at 375°. Freezes well. Kids love these soft, moist raisin spice bars.

Peanut Butter Chocolate Chip Cookies

Yields 3 dozen

1½ cups flour
1 tsp. baking soda
½ cup butter, softened
½ cup (packed) brown
    sugar
½ cup sugar
1 egg
½ tsp. vanilla
½ cup smooth peanut
    butter
1 cup chocolate chips

Preheat oven to 375°. Sift flour and soda. Cream butter and sugars until light and fluffy. Mix in egg, vanilla and peanut butter. Mix in dry ingredients, then add chocolate chips. Form dough into 1-inch balls. Arrange on ungreased baking sheet, spacing 1½ inches apart. Flatten to thickness of ½-inch with back of fork dipped in sugar. Bake 12 minutes or until golden.

Note: Freezes well.

Chocolate Cookies

Yields 5 dozen

1½ cup butter or margarine
3 cups sugar
1 T. vanilla
3 eggs
6 squares (1-oz. each) chocolate, melted
5¼ cups flour
¾ tsp. baking soda
1 cup buttermilk

Preheat oven to 350°. Cream butter and sugar, add vanilla and eggs. Beat well. Add chocolate and mix. Combine flour and soda; add alternately with milk. Drop by tsp. onto cookie sheet. Bake 12 to 15 minutes.
Note: Freezes well.

Coconut Joys

Yields 3 dozen

½ cup butter or margarine
2 cups powdered sugar
3 cups (8-oz.) coconut chocolate chips or Maraschino cherry slices

Melt butter in saucepan or microwave. Add sugar and coconut. Mix well. Shape into small balls and place on cookie sheet. Top with chocolate chip or cherry slice. Chill until firm. Store in refrigerator.
Note: Freezes well. This is an easy, no bake, pretty cookie.

German Chocolate Bars

Yields 4 dozen

4 oz. German chocolate
¼ cup butter or margarine
1 14-oz. can sweetened condensed milk, divided
2 eggs
½ cup biscuit mix
1 tsp. vanilla
7 oz. flaked coconut
1 cup chopped pecans

Preheat oven to 325°. Grease 9 x 13-inch baking pan. Melt chocolate and butter. Add ½ cup sweetened condensed milk, eggs, biscuit mix and vanilla. Spread in pan. Mix remaining milk and coconut. Spoon over chocolate. Top with pecans. Bake 25 minutes. Cool and cut into bars.

Grand Grahams

Yields 2 dozen

24 large graham crackers
 1 cup butter
 1 cup (packed) brown
     sugar
½ cup chocolate chips

Preheat oven to 350°. Arrange crackers on cookie sheets in single layer. Combine butter and sugar in saucepan and boil for 2 minutes. Spread mixture on crackers, top with chips and bake for 10 minutes.

Note: So easy children love to make them.

Variation: Substitute white sugar for brown and top with ¼ cup chopped almonds.

Puff Pastry Cookie Sticks

Yields 3 dozen

 1 sheet Pepperidge Farm
     Puff Pastry
⅓ cup sugar
½ tsp. cinnamon

Preheat oven to 400°. Grease cookie sheet. On floured board, roll pastry to ⅛-inch thickness. Combine sugar and cinnamon and sprinkle on pastry. Cut pastry into thirds, then cut each third into 12 strips. Bake 20 minutes or until golden.

Note: Freezes well.

Forgotten Cookies

Yields 3 dozen

4 egg whites, room
   temperature
⅛ tsp. cream of tartar
1⅓ cups sugar
1 cup chopped pecans
2 cups chocolate chips
2 tsp. vanilla

Preheat oven to 350°. Beat egg whites and cream of tartar until foamy. Gradually add sugar and continue beating until stiff. Fold in pecans, chips and vanilla. Drop cookies by tsp. onto ungreased cookie sheet. Put cookies in oven and immediately turn off heat. Leave cookies in closed oven overnight.

No Bake Chocolate Cookies

Yields 3 dozen

2 cups sugar
5½ T. cocoa
½ cup milk
½ cup butter or margarine
3½ cups oatmeal
1 tsp. vanilla

Bring sugar, cocoa, milk, and butter to boil. Cook 1 minute and remove from heat. Add oatmeal and vanilla. Cool 15 minutes. Drop by tsp. on waxed paper. Cool and serve. *Note: Use ¼ cup peanut butter and ¼ butter instead of ½ cup butter for variety.*

Sfingi

Yields 2 dozen

2 eggs
¼ cup sugar
1 cup ricotta cheese
1½ cups flour
2 tsp. baking powder
   pinch of salt
¼ cup milk
½ tsp. cinnamon

Beat eggs and sugar until light. Add cheese, beat well. Mix in flour, baking powder, salt and milk. Blend well. Drop by teaspoonfuls into deep hot oil for about 2 to 3 minutes, turning once. Roll in powdered sugar.

New Mexico Mocha Balls   Yields 6 dozen

1 cup butter
½ cup sugar
2 tsp. vanilla extract
1¾ cups flour
¼ cup cocoa
1 T. instant coffee
½ tsp. salt
1 cup chopped nuts
½ cup chopped
   Maraschino cherries
powdered sugar

Cream butter, sugar and vanilla. Sift together flour, cocoa, coffee and salt; add to creamed mixture. Blend in nuts and cherries. Chill dough an hour for ease in handling. Preheat oven to 325°. Shape into 1-inch balls; place on baking sheets. Bake for 20 minutes. While warm, dust cookies with powdered sugar.

Pumpkin Pie Dessert Squares Yields 4 dozen

1 18½-oz. package yellow
   cake mix plus 2 T.
   flour
¾ cup butter, melted,
   divided
3 eggs
1 30-oz. can pumpkin
⅔ cup milk
¼ cup sugar
1 tsp. cinnamon

Preheat oven to 375°. Grease bottom only of 13 x 9 x 2-inch pan. Reserve 1 cup of cake mixture. Combine remaining cake mix, ½ cup butter and 1 egg. Press into bottom of pan. Prepare filling by combining pumpkin, milk and 2 eggs until smooth. Pour over crust. For topping: Combine reserved cake mix, sugar, cinnamon and ¼ cup butter. Sprinkle over filling. Bake 50 minutes, cool, cut into bars.

New Mexico Biscochito Shortbread

Yields 2 dozen

1 cup lard
2 cups flour
½ cup powdered sugar
2 tsp. anise seed
⅓ cup sugar
1 tsp. cinnamon

Preheat oven to 325°. Blend flour, powdered sugar and anise into lard just until mixed. Pat dough into ungreased 9 x 9-inch baking pan. Pierce dough with fork every ½ inch. Mix sugar and cinnamon; sprinkle on dough. Bake 25 minutes. Cut into bars while warm.

Note: Recipe needs lard for flavor. Freezes well. Easiest Biscochito west of the Rockies!

Shortbread Bars

Yields 2 dozen

2 cups flour
½ cup sugar
¾ cup butter or
    margarine, softened
1 T. cream
½ tsp. vanilla

Preheat oven to 350°. Grease cookie sheet. Combine all ingredients. Mix until dough can be formed. Flatten on greased cookie sheet to a 10 x 8-inch rectangle. Pierce with fork to make 2-inch squares. Do not separate. Bake for 20 minutes or until golden. Cut along pierce lines.

Note: For high altitude (5000 feet) increase cream to 2 T. and vanilla to 1 tsp. Bake at 375° for 20 minutes.

Variations: For Coffee Shortbread add 2 tsp. instant coffee and ¼ cup chopped pecans. For Almond Shortbread add ⅓ cup sliced almonds and ½ tsp. almond extract.

Gelatin Cookies

Yields 3 dozen

- 3 egg whites
- ¾ cup sugar
- 4 T. gelatin (any flavor)

Preheat oven to 300°. Cover 1 cookie sheet with brown paper. Whip egg whites until stiff peaks form. Add sugar and gelatin and re-whip until blended and peaks form. Drop batter on cookie sheet by tablespoonfuls about ½ inch apart. Bake 25 minutes. Do not open oven. Turn oven off and leave in hot oven for 20 more minutes. Remove and cool.

Note: Recipe may be doubled.

Frosted Coffee Bars

Yields 3 dozen

- ½ cup shortening
- 1 cup (packed) brown sugar
- 1 egg
- ½ cup strong coffee
- 2 cups flour
- ½ tsp. baking powder
- ½ tsp. baking soda
- ½ tsp. cinnamon
- ½ tsp. salt
- ½ cup raisins
- ¼ cup chopped walnuts
- 1½ cups powdered sugar
- 1 T. butter
- 3 T. strong coffee

Preheat oven to 375°. Grease 11 x 15-inch baking pan. Cream shortening with sugar; blend in egg and coffee. Add flour, baking powder, baking soda and spices, then raisins and walnuts. Spread in pan and bake for 15 minutes. When cooled, mix powdered sugar, butter and coffee. Frost bars.

Note: Freezes well.

Russian Tea Cake Bars

Yields 2 dozen

1   cup butter or margarine
½   cup powdered sugar
2   tsp. vanilla
½   tsp. salt
2   cups flour
1   cup chopped nuts

Preheat oven to 325°. Cream butter, sugar, vanilla and salt until fluffy. Blend in flour and nuts. Flatten on ungreased cookie sheet to a 9 x 6-inch rectangle. Cut into 1-inch squares. Do not separate. Bake for 25 minutes or until golden. Cut into squares. Cool 5 minutes; roll in additional powdered sugar. *Note: For high altitude (5000 feet) bake at 350°. Freezes well.*

Tempting Tassies

Yields 4 dozen

1   cup plus 2 tsp. butter, divided
1   8-oz. package cream cheese
2   cups flour
    dash of salt
2   eggs, lightly beaten
1½ cups (packed) brown sugar
1   cup chopped pecans, walnuts, chopped dates, mincemeat or coconut

Blend 1 cup butter, cheese, flour and salt with pastry blender. Chill. Form into small balls and put into muffin tin to make small tarts. The 1¾-inch muffin tins work beautifully. Preheat oven to 375°. Mix eggs, 2 tsp. melted butter and sugar. Add nuts, or desired fruit. Mix well to blend. Fill individual tarts ½ full with filling. Bake for 15 minutes. Let tassies cool in pans before removing. *Note: These may be stored in the refrigerator as long as a week or frozen. Delicious!*

Soft Date Bars

Yields 3 dozen

CRUST:
- ¾ cup butter
- 1 cup (packed) brown sugar
- 1¾ cups flour
- ½ tsp. baking soda
- 1½ cups rolled oats

FILLING:
- 3 cups chopped dates
- ¼ cup sugar
- 1½ cups water

Preheat oven to 375°. To make crust mix butter and sugar. Blend in flour, soda and oats. Pat half of mixture into bottom of greased 13 x 9-inch baking pan. In saucepan, combine filling ingredients. Cook 10 minutes until thickened, stirring occasionally. Spread filling mixture on crumb crust, and top with remaining crumbs. Bake 30 minutes until golden. *Note: Add ½ cup chopped pecans to filling, if desired. Freezes well. Delicious!*

Sugar Cookie Bars

Yields 4 dozen

- 1½ cups flour
- ½ cup sugar
- ½ cup butter or margarine, softened
- 2 T. orange juice
- 1 egg
- 1 tsp. baking powder
- ½ tsp. salt
- 1 tsp. vanilla

Preheat oven to 350°. Grease 9 x 13-inch pan. Combine all ingredients. Beat until blended, 1 minute. Spread in pan and sprinkle with additional sugar. Bake for 25 minutes or until golden. Cool 5 minutes. Cut into squares. *Note: For high altitude (5000 feet), bake at 375°. Decrease baking powder to ¾ tsp. These sugar cookies may be served plain, topped with fancy sugar or frosted. Freezes well.*

Spicy Shortbread

Yields 16

1 cup flour
¼ cup (packed) brown sugar
2 T. plus 1½ tsp. cornstarch
½ tsp. cinnamon
½ cup butter
½ tsp. vanilla
½ cup (2-oz.) chopped pecans

Preheat oven to 375°. Mix flour, sugar, cornstarch and cinnamon. Add butter and vanilla; cut into flour until mixture resembles coarse meal. Add pecans. Press dough to fit base of 11-inch ungreased tart pan. Cut into 16 wedges. Pierce with fork. Bake 20 minutes until shortbread is golden. Recut wedges. Cool in pan on rack.

Toffee Squares

Yields 5 dozen

1 cup butter
1 cup (packed) dark brown sugar
pinch of salt
1 egg
2 cups flour
1 tsp. vanilla
1 cup chocolate chips
½ chopped nuts

Preheat oven to 350°. Grease 11 x 15-inch pan. To make toffee mix butter, sugar, salt, egg, flour and vanilla. Spread in pan and bake for 20 minutes. Melt chocolate chips and spread on toffee as soon as it is removed from the oven; top with nuts. Cut into squares immediately.

Rum Balls

Yields 3 dozen

2¼ cups vanilla wafer crumbs
1 cup powdered sugar
2 T. cocoa
1 cup chopped nuts
¼ cup corn syrup
¼ cup rum

Mix all ingredients thoroughly. Chill in refrigerator for 1 hour, then shape into balls and roll in powdered or granulated sugar. Store in airtight container at least 3 days.

Black Forest Bars   Yields 36

1   18½-oz. fudge cake mix
1   21-oz. can cherry pie
    filling
1   tsp. almond extract
2   eggs, beaten
1   cup sugar
5   T. butter or margarine
⅓   cup milk
6   oz. (1 cup) chocolate
    chips
18 Maraschino cherries,
    cut in half

Preheat oven to 350°. Grease 9 x 13-inch pan. In large bowl, stir by hand cake mix, pie filling, extract and eggs. Pour into prepared baking pan and bake for 25 minutes or until done. Remove from oven and cool. Cut into bars. Remove from pan. Place on waxed paper or wire rack. FROSTING: In small saucepan combine sugar, butter and milk; bring to a boil, stirring constantly for 1 minute. Remove from heat; stir in chips and blend until smooth. Top individual bars with frosting and cherry.

Note: Freezes well. Delicious!

Pecan Pie Squares   Yields 9

1   cup plus 1 T. flour
½   cup rolled oats
¾   cup (packed) brown
    sugar, divided
½   cup butter or margarine
3   eggs
¾   cup light corn syrup
1   cup broken pecans
1   tsp. vanilla
¼   tsp. salt

Preheat oven to 375°. Grease 9-inch square pan. Mix 1 cup flour, oats, ¼ cup brown sugar and butter until particles are fine. Press into bottom of pan. Bake 15 minutes. Beat eggs, syrup, pecans, vanilla, salt, ½ cup brown sugar and 1 T. flour. Pour over crust. Bake 25 minutes.

Variation: Substitute 1 cup coconut for pecans to make Southern Coconut Bars.

Almond Cheese Cake   Serves 12

2 cups graham cracker
    crumbs
1½ cups sugar, divided
½ cup butter, melted
1 lb. cream cheese,
    softened
2 eggs
3 tsp. almond extract,
    divided
2 cups sour cream

Preheat oven to 375°. Combine crumbs, ½ cup sugar and butter. Press into greased 10-inch springform pan. Beat cream cheese until smooth; blend in eggs, ⅔ cup sugar and 1 tsp. almond extract. Pour over crust and bake for 20 minutes. Combine sour cream, remainder of sugar and 2 tsp. extract. Carefully spread over baked filling. Return to 425° oven for 10 minutes. Cool, then chill to serve.

Note: Freezes well. This is very nice topped with fruit or Simply Splendid Chocolate Sauce, found in this book.

Banana Split Cake   Serves 12

1½ cup butter, divided
2 cups graham cracker
    crumbs
2 eggs
1 lb. powdered sugar
¾ cup chopped nuts,
    divided
5 bananas, sliced
1 20-oz. can crushed
    pineapple, well
    drained
1 pint whipping cream or
    CoolWhip
12 Maraschino cherries

Melt ½ cup butter and combine with crumbs. Pat into bottom of 9 x 13 inch pan. Combine 1 cup butter, eggs and sugar. Mix well and spread over crumb mixture. Sprinkle with ½ cup nuts. Arrange bananas over mixture and top with pineapple. Whip cream, spread over all and top with cherries and remaining nuts. Refrigerate for at least 3 hours.

Ambrosia Angel Cake   Serves 10

1   6-oz. box strawberry
      gelatin
1½ pints whipping cream,
      divided
¾   cup powdered sugar,
      divided
1   large angel cake, day
      old, torn into bite-
      size pieces
1   quart strawberries,
      hulled and quartered

Day before: Prepare strawberry gelatin per package instructions, refrigerate to set. Whip 1 pint cream with ½ cup powdered sugar until soft peaks form. Stir set gelatin with fork. In large bowl combine gelatin, whipped cream, strawberries and cake. Blend gently by hand, leaving clumps of gelatin. Place mixture into ungreased angel cake pan. Press gently, cover and chill overnight. Invert onto serving plate. Whip ½ pint whipping cream with ¼ cup powdered sugar and frost cake. Garnish with whole strawberries and leaves. Serve chilled.

Note: You'll get raves from guests and children on this do-ahead dessert.

Coconut Cake   Serves 8

2   8- or 9-inch layers of
      yellow cake, baked
      and cooled
2   cups sour cream
1   tsp. vanilla
5   cups shredded coconut
1   cup powdered sugar

Mix sour cream, vanilla and coconut. Add sugar to coconut mixture and blend well. Frost cake. Garnish with additional toasted coconut if desired.

Note: A simple coconut lover's cake.

Buccilata Cake

Serves 8 to 10

½ cup butter or margarine
1½ cups sugar
2 eggs separated
3½ cups flour
1 T. baking powder
1¼ cups milk
½ cup whiskey
3 T. anise seed

Preheat oven to 350°. Cream butter and sugar. Beat egg whites until stiff. Add egg yolks to butter mixture. Add remaining ingredients. Fold in egg whites. Bake in Bundt pan for 50 minutes or until golden. Sprinkle with powdered sugar. Cool.
Note: Freezes well. This cake is a MUST for anise lovers.

Coconut Sour Cream Torte

Serves 12

1 cup butter or margarine, softened
3 cups sugar, divided
4 large eggs, room temperature
3¼ cups flour
1 tsp. baking powder
1 cup milk
1 tsp. vanilla
1 cup sour cream
1 7-oz. package flaked coconut

Preheat oven to 350°. Cream butter and 2 cups of sugar until light and fluffy. Add eggs, one at a time, beating well after each addition. Sift together flour and baking powder. Add alternately with milk, stir in vanilla. Pour into 2 greased 9-inch cake pans. Bake 30 minutes or until cake tests done. Cool 5 minutes. Remove from pans and place on rack until cool. Split each layer in ½ horizontally. Combine sour cream and remaining sugar. Stir in coconut. Spread between layers and on top of cake. Refrigerate until serving.

Eleven Minute Carrot Cake
Serves 10

1½ cups flour
2 tsp. cinnamon
1½ tsp. baking soda
1 tsp. nutmeg
3 cups grated carrots
1½ cups sugar
1 cup oil
1¼ cup chopped walnuts,
       divided
3 eggs
1 8-oz. package cream
       cheese, softened
½ cup butter, softened
2 tsp. vanilla
3 cups powdered sugar

Lightly grease microwave safe tube pan. Sift together flour, cinnamon, soda and nutmeg. Combine carrots, sugar, oil, 1 cup walnuts and eggs; blend well. Add dry ingredients and mix thoroughly. Pour into tube pan. Microwave on high for 10 to 11 minutes, turning pan every 2 minutes. (Cake will pull away from pan.) Cool slightly before inverting onto serving plate. Whip cheese until smooth. Add butter and mix thoroughly. Add nuts and vanilla; blend well. Add powdered sugar and beat well. Frost cooled cake; garnish with additional walnuts, if desired.
Note: Freezes well.

Fresh Apple Cake
Serves 12 to 15

1 cup sugar
2 cups (packed) brown
       sugar, divided
½ cup plus 2 T. butter or
       margarine, divided
2 eggs
4 cups chopped apples
2 tsp. baking soda
4 tsp. cinnamon, divided
2½ cups plus 2 T. flour,
       divided
1 cup chopped nuts

Preheat oven to 375°. Grease 9 x 13-inch baking pan. Beat together sugar, 1 cup brown sugar, ½ cup butter and eggs. Add apples, baking soda, 2 tsp. cinnamon, and 2½ cups flour. Pour into pan. Mix together, 1 cup brown sugar, 2 tsp. cinnamon, 2 T. flour, 2 T. butter and nuts. Sprinkle on cake. Bake for 45 minutes.
Note: Freezes well.

Chocolate Torte
Serves 12

1   9 x 5-inch pound cake
1   8-oz. package cream
    cheese, softened
4   1-oz. squares semisweet
    chocolate
1   oz. almond liqueur
1½ cups raspberry jam
2   cups chocolate frosting

Slice cake horizontally into 3, ½-inch slices. Place bottom layer of cake on serving platter. Beat cheese until smooth. Chop chocolate into fine bits in blender. Mix chocolate bits with liqueur and jam. Spread bottom layer with half of cheese, top with half of raspberry mixture. Repeat, using remaining cake, cheese and raspberry mixture. Frost cake with chocolate frosting. Refrigerate until serving.

Note: This is an outstanding torte. Freezes well.

Cream Cheese Pound Cake
Serves 12 to 16

1   8-oz. package cream
    cheese, softened
1½ cups butter, softened
3   cups sugar
6   eggs
3   cups cake flour
2   tsp. almond extract

Preheat oven to 350°. Grease 12 cup tube pan. Beat cheese, butter and sugar in bowl until smooth. Add eggs one at a time alternately with flour, stirring after each addition. Blend in extract. Pour batter into pan. Bake 30 minutes. Reduce temperature to 325° and continue baking 45 minutes or until tester inserted near center comes out clean. Cool in pan on rack. Serve.

Note: Freezes well. This cake converts nicely into a torte.

Microwave Chocolate Cherry Cake

Serves 8

1 18 oz. package Devil's Food Cake mix
1 21-oz. can cherry pie filling
3 eggs, beaten
½ cup chocolate chips
1 T. butter or margarine
2 T. milk
½ cup powdered sugar

Grease 12-cup microwave safe tube pan. Blend cake mix, pie filling and eggs and beat 2 minutes. Pour into pan. Microwave on high for 13 minutes, rotating pan ¼ turn every 3 minutes. Cool. Combine chips, butter and milk in microwave safe container. Microwave on high for 1 minute or until chips melt. Stir in sugar and frost cake.

Microwave Oatmeal Cake

Serves 8

¾ cup boiling water
¾ cup rolled oats
1 18-oz. package German Chocolate Cake mix
¾ cup hot coffee
⅓ cup oil
3 eggs
½ cup chopped nuts
1 cup powdered sugar
2 T. cocoa
1½ oz. cream cheese, softened
2 tsp. vanilla

Grease and sugar 12-cup microwave safe tube pan. Pour boiling water over oats and set aside. Blend cake mix, coffee, oil and eggs and beat 2 minutes. Add oat mixture and nuts to batter and blend well. Pour into pan. Microwave on high for 11 minutes, rotating pan ¼ turn every 3 minutes. Cool in pan for 5 minutes. Remove from pan and cool completely. Combine sugar, cocoa, cheese, and vanilla. Frost cake.

Million Dollar Cake

Serves 12 to 15

1 18½-oz. box butter cake
    mix
1 cup butter or
    margarine, melted
5 eggs
1 8-oz. package cream
    cheese
1 1-lb. box powdered
    sugar
1 cup chopped pecans

Preheat oven to 350°. Grease and flour 13 x 9-inch baking pan. Mix dry cake mix, melted butter and 3 eggs. Spread batter in pan. Mix cream cheese, powdered sugar (reserve ¼ cup) and 2 eggs. Pour over cake batter, sealing around edges. Sprinkle pecans over this and bake for 40 minutes. When cool, sprinkle with remaining powdered sugar.

Note: Quick, easy and rich!

Raspberry Cake

Serves 8

CRUST:
1½ cups flour
 ½ cup sugar
 1 tsp. baking powder
 ½ cup butter
 1 egg
 ½ cup raspberry jam,
       divided
FILLING:
 ½ cup butter
 ⅔ cup sugar
 ½ tsp. almond extract
 2 eggs
 1 cup ground almonds
FROSTING:
 ½ cup powdered sugar
 2 tsp. lemon juice

Grease 9 x 1½-inch spring-form pan. Blend flour, sugar and baking powder. Blend in butter, mix in egg. Press dough evenly on bottom of pan. Spread ¼ cup jam over dough. Cover and chill.
FILLING: Cream butter, sugar and extract. Add eggs, beating well. Stir in almonds. Spoon filling on top of crust. Bake at 350° for 50 minutes. Cool in pan, remove cake carefully. Spread remaining ¼ cup jam over the top. FROSTING: Mix powdered sugar and lemon juice. Drizzle over top of jam.
Note: Freezes well.

Rio Grande Mud Cake
Serves 12 to 15

1½ cups margarine,
       softened
2   cups sugar
4   eggs
1   tsp. vanilla
1½ cup flour
2   T. plus ⅓ cup cocoa
1   cup pecans
1   7-oz. jar marshmallow
       creme
1   lb. powdered sugar
½   cup evaporated milk
1   tsp. vanilla

Preheat oven to 350°. Grease 9 x 13-inch pan. Cream 1 cup margarine and sugar. Add eggs and vanilla. Mix well. Add flour, nuts and 2 T. cocoa. Beat 2 minutes. Bake for 25 minutes. Spread marshmallow cream on hot cake. Cool. Mix powdered sugar, ½ cup margarine, evaporated milk, ⅓ cup cocoa and vanilla. Beat until fluffy. Frost cake.
Note: Freezes well.

Rocky Mountain Cake
Serves 12 to 15

2   cups flour
1¾ cups sugar
¼   tsp. salt
½   cup cocoa, divided
1   cup water
1   cup margarine
½   cup salad oil
½   cup plus ⅓ cup
       buttermilk
2   eggs
1   tsp. baking soda
1   lb. powdered sugar
½   tsp. vanilla
¼   cup chopped nuts
½   cup miniature
       marshmallows

Preheat oven to 400°. Grease 11 x 15-inch pan. Sift flour, sugar, salt and ¼ cup cocoa. In saucepan bring to boil water, ½ cup margarine, and salad oil. Pour over dry ingredients and beat until creamy. Add ½ cup buttermilk, eggs and baking soda. Beat well and bake for 18 minutes. Bring ½ cup margarine, ¼ cup cocoa and ⅓ cup buttermilk to boil, stirring constantly. Remove from heat. Add powdered sugar and vanilla. Beat until smooth. Add nuts and marshmallows. Spread on hot cake.
Note: Freezes well.

Rum Cake

Serves 8 to 10

1 18-oz. package yellow
   cake mix
½ cup rum
½ cup vegetable oil
½ cup water
4 eggs
SAUCE:
¼ cup butter
½ cup sugar
⅛ cup water
⅛ cup rum

Preheat oven to 325°. Grease tube pan. Mix cake mix, rum, oil and water. Beat in eggs one at a time. Pour into pan, bake 60 minutes. For sauce, combine butter, sugar, ⅛ cup water and rum in saucepan. Boil for 3 minutes. Pour hot sauce over hot cake. Let stand 30 minutes. Invert onto serving platter. Serve warm or cold, plain, powdered sugared or with whipped cream.
Note: Freezes well.

Prune Cake

Serves 10

1 cup sour milk
1 tsp. baking soda
1½ cups sugar
3 eggs
⅔ cups oil
1 cup mashed prunes,
   cooked
1 cup nuts
2 cups flour
1 tsp. salt
1 tsp. cloves
1 tsp. cinnamon
1 tsp. nutmeg

Preheat oven to 350°. Grease Bundt pan. Combine sour milk and soda. Beat sugar and eggs. Add oil, prunes, nuts, milk mixture, flour and spices. Batter will be thin. Pour into pan, bake 40 minutes or until done.
Note: To sour milk, add 1 tsp. vinegar to 1 cup of milk. To cook prunes, add 1 cup of water to 1 cup of prunes and simmer 2 minutes. Cake freezes well.

Java-Rum Torte   **Serves 8 to 10**

½ cup sugar
½ cup water
2 T. instant coffee
2 T. rum
1 T. butter or margarine
1 10¾-oz. frozen pound
    cake, thawed
1 envelope dessert
    topping mix, whipped

To make Java mixture, combine sugar, water and coffee in saucepan. Boil for 3 minutes, stirring occasionally. Remove from heat; stir in rum and butter. Cool 5 minutes. Slice cake lengthwise into 3 layers. Spoon 3 T. of the Java mixture over bottom layer. Spread with ⅓ of the prepared topping. Invert second layer and spoon 3 T. of Java mixture on bottom side. Place Java side down on top of bottom layer, spoon another 3 T. of Java on top of middle layer, along with ⅓ of the topping. Spoon 3 T. Java on bottom surface of top layer; invert and place atop stack. Spread remaining topping on top. Drizzle Java over top of torte.

Note: Freezes well. Easy to make with purchased pound cake.

Plum Pudding with Hard Sauce

Serves 12 to 16

FOR PUDDING:
- 1 cup flour
- 1 tsp. baking soda
- dash salt
- 1 tsp. cinnamon
- ¼ tsp. nutmeg
- ½ tsp. allspice
- 1½ cups raisins
- 2 cups prunes, diced
- ¼ tsp. lemon peel
- ¼ tsp. orange peel
- ½ cup chopped walnuts
- 1½ cups soft bread crumbs
- ¾ cup brown sugar
- ¼ cup molasses
- ¾ cup cranberry sauce
- 1 cup butter
- 3 eggs
- ¼ cup brandy

FOR HARD SAUCE:
- ½ cup butter, soft
- 1 cup powdered sugar
- ½ tsp. vanilla or rum flavoring

Grease tube or Bundt pan generously. Sift flour, soda, salt, cinnamon, nutmeg and allspice. Blend in remaining ingredients. Pour into pan and steam (place pan in deep well cooker or kettle with tight fitting lid) for about 6 hours. Serve hot with hard sauce.

For Hard Sauce: Beat butter and sugar until fluffy, stir in flavoring. Chill about 1 hour. (Yields ¾ cup hard sauce.)

Note: This is very rich, so serve small pieces. Keeps well in refrigerator for at least a week. Freezes well.

Pumpkin Cheesecake   Serves 12

CRUST:
- ¾ cup graham cracker crumbs
- ½ cup finely chopped pecans
- ¼ cup (packed) brown sugar
- ¼ cup granulated sugar
- ¼ cup melted butter

FILLING:
- 24 oz. cream cheese, softened
- 1 cup plus 2 T. granulated sugar
- 2 T. cream
- 1 tsp. vanilla
- 1 cup canned pumpkin
- 3 large eggs
- 1½ tsp. cinnamon
- ½ tsp. nutmeg
- ½ tsp. ground ginger
- ½ tsp. salt
- 1 tsp. cornstarch

CRUST: Combine crumbs, pecans, sugars and butter. Press into the bottom of a 10-inch springform pan. Freeze for 15 minutes.

FILLING: Cream the cream cheese with half the sugar. Beat in the cream and vanilla. Stir the cornstarch into the spices. Add to cream cheese mixture along with pumpkin and eggs and remaining sugar. Pour the filling into the pan containing the frozen crust. Bake in preheated 350° oven for 40 to 45 minutes. Place pan on a rack and cool to room temperature. Chill, loosely covered, overnight. Slice into wedges.

Note: Delicious garnished with whipped cream flavored with rum instead of vanilla.

Popcorn Cake   Yields 1 cake or 36 cupcakes

- ¼ cup butter or margarine
- ¼ cup oil
- ½ lb. marshmallows
- 20 caramels
- 10 cups popped corn
- ½ lb. salted peanuts
- ½ lb. M & M's candy

Oil 12 cup tube pan. Melt butter, oil, marshmallows and caramels. Mix popcorn and peanuts. Add melted ingredients and stir to coat. Add M & M's last. Press into pan. Let stand until firm and cool. Remove from pan.

Note: A sure hit at a children's party.

Mock Eclair Torte   **Serves 8 to 10**

1 **18.25-oz. package yellow cake mix**
1 **3-oz. package instant pudding mix**
   chocolate fudge topping

Mix cake as directed on package. Bake in two greased 8 x 5-inch loaf pans 25 to 35 minutes. Cool. Mix pudding according to package directions. Remove cake from pans. Slice each cake into thirds, lengthwise. Place the bottom layer on serving dish. Spread one-forth of the pudding on bottom layer. Top with second layer and repeat with one-fourth of pudding. Place last layer on top of torte and generously top with chocolate fudge topping, allowing it to drizzle down sides of torte. Repeat process on a separate dish for the second torte. Refrigerate and serve cold, sliced as bread, in 1-inch pieces.

Note: Use purchased cake and canned pudding for an instant elegant dessert.

Strawberry Meringue Torte   Serves 8

½ cup butter, softened
1½ cups sugar, divided
4 large eggs, separated,
    room temperature
½ cup flour
1 tsp. baking powder
¼ cup milk
2 tsp. vanilla
¾ cup chopped walnuts
2 cups chilled whipping
    cream, whipped
1 cup sliced strawberries
1 cup whole strawberries

Preheat oven to 375°. Butter 2 8-inch cake pans with 2-inch high sides. Cream butter with ½ cup sugar. Blend in yolks. Stir together flour and baking powder; add to batter alternately with milk. Add vanilla. Pour into cake pans. With clean, dry beaters, beat egg whites until soft peaks form. Gradually add remaining 1 cup sugar and beat until stiff and shiny. Fold in nuts. Spread over cake batter. Bake until meringue is puffed and golden, 20 minutes. Cool. Remove one cake layer from pan and place onto platter, meringue side up. Spoon half of whipped cream over cake. Top with sliced strawberries. Place second cake layer over strawberries, meringue side up. Top with whipped cream and whole strawberries. Refrigerate until ready to serve.

Note: A very impressive dessert with a short preparation time. Can be made up to 4 hours ahead.

Chocolate Glaze   Frosts 1 cake

3 oz. unsweetened
   chocolate, chopped
1 cup cream
1 cup sugar
1 tsp. corn syrup
1 egg, beaten
1 tsp. vanilla

In saucepan combine chocolate, cream, sugar and corn syrup. Boil, stirring constantly, until temperature reaches 220°. Add 2 T. of this mixture to egg. Reduce heat to low and stir egg mixture into chocolate. Simmer for 4 minutes. Remove from heat, add vanilla and cool to room temperature. Place a filled layer cake on a wire rack over a jelly roll pan. Pour this glaze slowly over cake.
Note: Delicious!

French Silk Frosting   Frosts 2 9-inch layers

2⅔ cups powdered sugar
 ⅔ cup soft butter
 2 oz. melted unsweetened
   chocolate, cool
 ¾ tsp. vanilla
 2 T. milk

In small mixer bowl, blend sugar, butter, chocolate and vanilla on low speed. Gradually add milk, beat until smooth and fluffy.

Lemon Icing   Frosts 1 tube cake

1 lb. powdered sugar
½ cup butter, softened
3 T. lemon zest
½ cup lemon juice

Cream sugar and butter. Mix in zest and juice. Frost cake.
Note: Delicious on lemon or yellow cake.

Almond Crust Cherry Cream Pie Serves 8

½ cup chopped almonds
1 unbaked 9 or 10-inch
   pie shell
1 15-oz. can sweetened
   condensed milk
⅓ cup lemon juice
½ tsp. almond extract
1 tsp. vanilla
½ pint whipping cream,
   whipped
1 21-oz. can cherry pie
   filling

Preheat oven to 425°. Sprinkle almonds in pie crust and bake for 10 minutes or until golden. Combine condensed milk, lemon juice, extract, and vanilla. Stir until mixture thickens. Fold in whipped cream and spoon into cooled pie shell. Top with cherry pie filling. Chill 2 to 3 hours.

Note: This pie is very rich.

Best-in-the-West Lemon Meringue Pie

Serves 6

1 baked pie shell
4 whole eggs, separated
3 egg yolks
1 cup plus 2 T. sugar
¾ cup lemon juice
2 tsp. grated lemon rind
9 T. butter, softened
3 egg whites, at room
   temperature
¼ tsp. cream of tartar
¼ tsp. cornstarch
4 T. sugar
½ tsp. vanilla

In stainless steel bowl, combine egg yolks, 1 cup plus 2 T. sugar, lemon juice and rind. Place bowl over pot of boiling water and whisk over heat until mixture thickens, about 5 minutes. Do not boil. Remove from heat; whisk in butter until all is blended. Pour into pie shell; cool. Beat egg whites until foamy. Add cream of tartar and cornstarch. Beat until whites form soft peaks. Add 4 T. sugar and vanilla and beat until stiff. Spread over filling, sealing to edge of pastry. Bake at 350° until golden, about 10 minutes.

Note: To cut meringue easily, dip knife into water.

Chocolate Covered Cherries in a Pie

Serves 6 to 8

1   9-inch graham cracker
     pie shell, baked
1   cup semi-sweet
     chocolate chips
1   14-oz. can sweetened
     condensed milk
1   21-oz. can cherry pie
     filling
½   tsp. almond extract
8   Maraschino cherries

Place chips and milk in 1½-quart microwave safe bowl. Microwave on high for 2 minutes or until boiling. Stir until well blended. Mix in pie filling and extract. Pour into shell. Chill overnight. Garnish with cherries.

Note: The pie for chocolate covered cherry lovers.

Coconut Pecan Pie

Serves 6 to 8

1½ cups milk
1   cup sugar
1   cup coconut
½   cup flour
½   cup chopped pecans
¼   cup margarine or
     butter, softened
4   eggs
1½ tsp. vanilla extract
¾   tsp. baking powder
     toasted coconut
     whipped cream

Preheat oven to 325°. Grease 10-inch pie pan. Blend milk, sugar, 1 cup coconut, flour, pecans, butter, eggs, vanilla, and baking powder in blender until well combined. Pour into pan. Bake until golden and firm to touch, about 35 minutes. Sprinkle toasted coconut over top. Serve warm, passing whipped cream separately.

Dessert Pizza Pie

Serves 10 to 12

1   sugar cookie crust
1   8-oz. package cream
     cheese, softened
⅓   cup sugar
1   tsp. vanilla
     sliced fruits

Use your favorite sugar cookie recipe; put dough in pizza pan. Bake until done; cool. Blend cheese, sugar and vanilla; spread on crust. Top with colorful fresh fruits.

Creme de Menthe Pie   **Serves 6 to 8**

½ cup milk
18 large marshmallows
3 drops peppermint
   extract
3 T. Creme de Menthe
3 drops green food
   coloring
15 chocolate wafer cookies,
   crushed
1 cup whipped cream or
   topping

Heat milk and pour over marshmallows. Stir and let cool. Add extract, Creme de Menthe and food coloring. Crush cookies and mix so frosting will hold crumbs together. Set aside 2 T. of cookie crumbs. Place crumbs on bottom of 9-inch pie pan pressing to hold together. Add cream to marshmallow mixture. Pour into pan over crumbs and top with remaining crumbs. Refrigerate for several hours.

Rum Chiffon Pie   **Serves 8**

1 pie shell, baked
1 T. unflavored gelatin
¼ cup cold water
3 eggs separated
1½ cups milk
¾ cup sugar
⅛ tsp. salt
7 T. rum
½ pint whipping cream,
   whipped
¼ cup powdered sugar
½ tsp. vanilla

Soften gelatin in water for 5 minutes. Beat egg yolks. Add milk, sugar and salt and cook over low heat, stirring constantly. When mixture coats spoon, stir in gelatin and cool until mixture begins to thicken. Beat egg whites stiff. Fold into custard along with rum. Turn into pie shell. Whip cream until soft peaks form, then add sugar and vanilla and beat again until soft peaks form. Top pie with whipped cream and shaved chocolate if desired.

Margarita Pie

Serves 6 to 8

CRUST:
- ¾ cup pretzel crumbs
- ⅓ cup butter or margarine
- 3 T. sugar

FILLING:
- 1 envelope unflavored gelatin
- ½ cup lemon juice
- 4 eggs, separated
- 1 cup sugar, divided
- ¼ tsp. salt
- 1 tsp. grated lemon peel
- ⅓ cup tequila
- 3 T. Triple Sec

Grease 9-inch pie pan. Combine crumbs, butter, and 3 T. sugar; mix well. Press in bottom and sides of pan. Chill. To make filling, soften gelatin in lemon juice. Beat egg yolks in top half of double boiler; blend in ½ cup sugar, salt and lemon peel. Add softened gelatin. Cook over boiling water, stirring constantly, until thickened and gelatin is completely dissolved. Transfer to bowl; blend in tequila and Triple Sec. Chill until mixture is cold, but not further thickened. Beat egg whites until foamy; gradually beat in remaining ½ cup sugar until whites hold soft peaks. Pour cooked mixture slowly on egg whites, about ⅓ at a time, folding in carefully after each addition. Let stand until mixture mounds in spoon. Swirl into pie shell. Chill until set.

One Minute Pie

Serves 6

- 2 8-oz. cartons fruit yogurt, any flavor
- 1 8-oz. carton frozen whipped topping, thawed
- 1 graham cracker pie crust

Fold yogurt and topping together. Spoon into crust. Garnish as desired. Chill 1 hour.

Prize Pumpkin Pie   Serves 6 to 8

1 unbaked 9-inch pie
   shell
1 16-oz. can pumpkin
1 14-oz. can sweetened
   condensed milk
2 eggs
1 tsp. cinnamon
½ tsp. ginger
½ tsp. nutmeg
   whipped cream,
   optional

Preheat oven to 425°. Combine filling ingredients; mix well and pour into shell. Bake 15 minutes; reduce oven to 350° and continue baking 25 minutes or until knife inserted 1 inch from edge comes out clean. Cool. If desired, garnish with whipped cream. Refrigerate leftovers. *Note: This is so good, and easy to make that you'll want to serve it more frequently than just at Thanksgiving.*

Impossible French Apple Pie   Serves 6

STREUSEL:
1 cup biscuit mix
½ cup chopped nuts
⅓ cup (packed) brown
   sugar
3 T. butter or margarine
FILLING:
6 cups sliced pared tart
   apples
1¼ tsp. ground cinnamon
¼ tsp. ground nutmeg
1 cup sugar
¾ cup milk
½ cup biscuit mix
2 eggs
2 T. butter or margarine

Preheat oven to 325°. To make streusel, mix 1 cup biscuit mix, nuts, brown sugar and 3 T. of butter until crumbly. Set topping aside. Grease 10 inch pie plate. Mix apples and spices, turn into plate. Blend remaining ingredients; except streusel until smooth (15 seconds in blender on high). Pour into plate. Sprinkle with Streusel. Bake 1 hour or until knife inserted in center comes out clean.

Chocolate Nut Pie

Serves 6 to 8

FILLING:
- 6¼ oz. almond chocolate bars
- 17 large marshmallows
- ½ cup milk
- 1 cup cream, whipped

CRUST:
- 25 vanilla wafers, crushed
- ½ cup butter, softened

Melt chocolate, marshmallows and milk; cool. Fold in cream. Combine wafers and butter, press into 9-inch pie pan. Pour chocolate mixture into crust. Cover. Refrigerate.

Note: This chocolate lover's favorite keeps fresh up to 4 days. Top with shaved chocolate or whipped cream.

Rhubarb Custard Pie

Serves 8

- 3½ cups chopped rhubarb
- 1½ cups sugar
- 3 eggs, beaten
- ¼ cup half and half
- ⅛ tsp. salt
- 1 T. flour
- 1 8-inch unbaked pie shell

Preheat oven to 375°. Combine rhubarb, sugar, eggs, half and half and salt. Sprinkle flour over bottom of pie shell. Pour rubarb mixture into shell. Bake 1 hour or until set.

Note: Equally good with other tart fruit!

Sour Cream Peach Pie

Serves 6 to 8

- 1 9-inch unbaked pie shell
- ⅔ cup sugar
- 3 T. flour
- ½ tsp. cinnamon
- 4 cups sliced fresh peaches
- 1 cup sour cream
- ½ cup slivered almonds

Preheat oven to 375°. Combine sugar, flour and cinnamon. Gently add to peaches. Mix to coat. Add sour cream and combine well. Pour into pie shell. Top with almonds. Bake 40 minutes or until done.

SOUTHWEST SEASONS SOUTHWEST SEASONS SOUTHWEST SEASONS SOUTHWEST SEASONS SOUTHWEST

Millionaire Pie   **Serves 12 to 16**

2   cups powdered sugar
½   cup butter
1   tsp. vanilla
1   egg
2   baked 9 or 10-inch pie
     crusts
1½ cups drained crushed
     pineapple
¾   cup nuts
2   pints whipping cream,
     whipped, or Cool
     Whip

Cream powdered sugar and butter. Add vanilla and egg. Beat until light and fluffy. Spread mixture evenly into 2 pie crusts. Chill. Blend pineapple, nuts and whipped cream. Top butter mixture with whipped cream mixture and chill thoroughly.

Note: Pies may be made early in the day, covered and refrigerated.

Strawberry Pretzel Pie   **Serves 8**

1   cup crushed pretzels
2   T. sugar
6   T. butter or margarine,
     melted
4   oz. cream cheese,
     softened
½   cup powdered sugar
2   cups whipped cream or
     topping
1   3-oz. package
     strawberry gelatin
1   cup pineapple juice
1   10-oz. package frozen
     strawberries

Preheat oven to 350°. Mix together pretzels, sugar and butter. Spread in 8 or 9 inch pie plate. Bake for 10 minutes. Cool. For first layer of filling mix cream cheese, sugar and whipped cream. Beat until smooth and spread over crust. Refrigerate. For top layer, bring pineapple juice to a boil, dissolve gelatin in it and add strawberries. Chill 1 hour. Spread over cream cheese layer. Refrigerate 4 hours or until set.

Note: This pretty, do ahead pie is easy to make and very good.

Ritzy Pie

Serves 8

20 Ritz crackers, crushed
¾ cup broken pecans
1 cup plus 1 T. sugar
3 egg whites, beaten stiff
½ pint whipping cream

Preheat oven to 350°. Grease 9-inch pie pan. Combine crumbs, nuts, and ½ cup sugar. Add remaining ½ cup sugar to egg white. Fold nut mixture into egg whites. Put into pan; bake for 20 minutes; cool. Whip cream, add 1 T. sugar. Spread on pie 4 hours before serving.

Shoo-Fly Pie

Serves 6 to 8

1 cup flour
⅔ cup (packed) brown sugar
1 T. butter
1 cup dark molasses
¾ cup plus 2 T. boiling water
1 tsp. baking soda
1 egg, beaten
1 pie shell, uncooked

Preheat oven to 375°. Mix flour, brown sugar and butter until crumbed. Set aside ½ of the mixture. Mix (do NOT beat) molasses, water, soda and egg with remaining crumbs. Put in pie shell. Cover with reserved crumbs. Bake for 11 minutes, then reduce heat to 350° and bake an additional 30 minutes.

Impossible Pecan Pie

Serves 6

1½ cups chopped pecans
¾ cup brown sugar
¾ cup milk
¾ cup light corn syrup
½ cup biscuit mix
¼ cup margarine
4 eggs
1½ tsp. vanilla

Preheat oven to 350°. Butter 9-inch pie pan. Sprinkle pecans in pan. Blend remaining ingredients in blender until smooth. Pour into pan. Bake 50 minutes or until knife inserted near center comes out clean.

Baklava   Yields 24 to 30

2 cups chopped walnuts
2½ cup sugar
1 T. cinnamon
⅛ tsp. ground cloves
1 lb. phyllo sheets
1 to 2 lb. butter
1 cup honey
2 cups water
⅛ tsp. lemon rind
1 cinnamon stick

Preheat oven to 350°. Mix nuts, ½ cup sugar, cinnamon and cloves. Brush 9 x 13-inch baking pan with melted butter. Place 2 phyllo sheets in bottom of pan and brush with butter. Repeat layering twice. Spread nuts evenly over sheets. Continue layering and buttering as above with remaining phyllo. With sharp knife, cut pastry into diamond shapes. Pour remaining butter over pan. Bake 1 hour or until golden and puffy. In saucepan combine honey, water, 2 cups of sugar, rind and cinnamon stick. Boil syrup for 10 minutes. Slowly pour hot syrup over hot baklava. Cool, refrigerate or freeze. Serve chilled.

Flaming Peach Melba   Serves 8

¾ cup raspberry jam
1 28-oz. can sliced
      peaches, drained
1 T. lemon juice
¼ cup brandy
¼ cup rum
      ice cream

Melt jam in microwave. Add peaches and lemon juice. Heat through. Put all in chafing dish. Keep hot. Warm brandy and rum, pour over peach mixture, ignite. Serve flaming, over ice cream.
Note: "Wow" your guests with this easy flaming treat.

Apple Crumble

Serves 6

4 cups sliced, pared, cored cooking apples
¾ cup (packed) brown sugar
½ cup flour
½ cup rolled oats
¾ tsp. cinnamon
¾ tsp. nutmeg
⅓ cup butter, softened

Preheat oven to 375°. Place apples in greased 8-inch square baking dish. Blend remaining ingredients until crumbly. Sprinkle over apples. Bake 30 minutes or until golden.

Note: Very good served warm with ice cream. Almost any fruit can be substituted for apples. Adjust sugar accordingly.

Cream Puffs

Yields 10

½ cup butter or margarine
1 cup boiling water
1 cup flour
4 eggs
Almond Custard filling

Preheat oven to 400°. Heat water and butter to boil. Add flour and stir vigorously over low heat 1 minute, until mixture forms a ball. Remove from heat. Beat in eggs thoroughly, 1 at a time, until smooth. Drop by spoon onto ungreased baking sheet into 10 mounds 3 inches apart. Bake 45 minutes until golden and puffy. Cool. Cut off tops, fill and replace tops. Fill with Almond Custard Filling (see index), dust top with powdered sugar and top with cherry.

Note: Beautiful and delicious! Make 3 dozen small puffs and fill with a sandwich filling (see index) for appetizers.

Bananas Flambe   Serves 8

1   **quart vanilla ice cream**
½   **cup butter or margarine**
⅔   **cup (packed) brown
      sugar**
1   **tsp. cinnamon**
4   **firm bananas**
⅓   **cup light rum**

Scoop ice cream into dessert dishes and place in freezer until serving. In chafing dish heat butter, sugar and cinnamon for 3 minutes. Cut bananas diagonally into ½-inch slices and place in chafing dish. Gently turn bananas to coat with sugar mixture. In microwave heat rum on high for 10 seconds. Pour over bananas and ignite. Spoon sauce and bananas over ice cream and serve immediately.

Black Bolivian   Serves 8

8   **T. butter**
8   **ripe bananas, sliced**
¾   **cup coffee flavored
      liqueur**
1   **quart dark chocolate ice
      cream**
    sliced almonds
    whipped cream

Up to one day in advance, scoop ice cream into stemmed sherbet glasses. Freeze. When ready to serve, melt butter in chafing dish. Add bananas and saute until browned and slightly sticky. Pour liqueur over bananas. Ignite; when flames subside, ladle over ice cream. Garnish with whipped cream and almonds.
Note: An easy dessert for elegant tableside preparation.

Blushing Apple-Cheese Tart   Serves 4 to 6

1 **sheet Pepperidge Farm Puff Pastry**
2 **cups peeled, sliced cooking apples**
½ **cup oatmeal**
½ **cup (packed) brown sugar**
¾ **cup grated Cheddar cheese**
¼ **cup red hots**

Preheat oven to 375°. Combine apples, oats, sugar and red hots. Roll pastry to ⅛ inch thickness. Pour mixture in center of pastry and top with cheese. Fold pastry (as envelope) press to seal, bake for 25 minutes or until done.
Note: Freezes well.

Flaming Cherries Jubilee   Serves 8

1 **quart vanilla ice cream**
¾ **cup currant jelly**
1 **16-oz. can pitted dark sweet cherries, drained**
¼ **cup rum**
¼ **cup brandy**

Scoop ice cream into dessert dishes and freeze until ready to serve. Melt jelly in microwave on high for 1 minute. Stir in cherries and transfer to chafing dish. Heat through. Heat rum and brandy in microwave on high for 20 seconds. Pour over cherries, ignite and serve flaming over ice cream.

Ice Cream Dream   Serves 6

3 **oz. brandy**
3 **oz. creme de cacao**
1½ **oz. orange-flavored liqueur**
1 **quart vanilla ice cream**

Combine brandy and liqueurs in blender; add vanilla ice cream a scoop at a time, blending just until smooth. Serve at once in stemmed glasses or place in freezer until served.

Forgotten Dessert

Serves 12 to 15

- 6 **egg whites, room temperature**
- ½ **tsp. cream of tartar**
- ¼ **tsp. salt**
- 2 **cups sugar, divided**
- 2 **tsp. vanilla**
- 8 **oz. cream cheese, softened**
- 1 **pint whipping cream**
- 2 **cups miniature marshmallows**
- 1 **20-oz. can cherry pie filling**

Preheat oven to 425°. Beat egg whites and cream of tartar until stiff. Add salt, 1½ cups sugar and 1 tsp. vanilla. Spread meringue in 9 x 13-inch baking pan. Put in oven and turn oven OFF. Keep door closed and leave in oven overnight. Next day, whip cream, and mix with cream cheese, ½ cup sugar, vanilla and marshmallows. Spread on meringue and refrigerate overnight. To serve, cut, place on dessert plates and top with cherries. *Note: Simple and delicious!*

Magnificent Mousse

Serves 8 to 10

- 2 **cups chocolate chips**
- 1 **cup whipping cream, scalding hot**
- 3 **eggs**
- 3 **T. brandy, rum, or liqueur**

In blender blend chips, cream, eggs and flavoring. Pour into dessert dishes and chill several hours until set. Top with whipped cream. *Note: Can be prepared 24 hours in advance and refrigerated or frozen.*

Rhubarb Sauce

Serves 4

- 4 **cups rhubarb cut in 1-inch pieces**
- 1 **cup sugar**
- 1 **cup water**

Combine all ingredients in saucepan. Cover and simmer for 10 minutes. Store refrigerated.

Individual Baked Alaskas Serves 4

4 paper baking cups, flattened
4 pound cake slices
4 egg whites
½ tsp. cream of tartar
½ cup sugar
4 scoops ice cream
4 sugar cubes, soaked with brandy

Cut cake slices slightly smaller than papers. Put cake slices on papers, and ice cream on cake slices. Make meringue by beating egg whites, cream of tartar and sugar until soft peaks form. Cover cake and ice cream with meringue. Seal to paper. Bake at 450° for 2 minutes, or until golden. Serve immediately or return to freezer, uncovered for up to 24 hours. If frozen, let stand at room temperature 10 minutes before serving. Top with brandy-soaked sugar cube, ignite, and serve flaming.
Note: Recipe may be doubled, tripled, etc.

Pineapple Orange Creme Serves 4 to 6

1 cup graham cracker crumbs, reserve 5 T.
4 T. butter
½ cup dry milk
½ cup orange juice
1 egg white
1 T. lemon juice
4 T. sugar
1 8-oz. can crushed pineapple, drained

Combine crumbs and butter. Press into 8-inch pan. Beat milk, juice and egg white on high speed for 3 minutes. Add lemon juice and beat 3 more minutes on high speed. Blend in sugar for 30 seconds. Fold in pineapple. Pour over crumbs. Sprinkle reserved crumbs on top. Freeze 8 hours or overnight.

Peking Almond Float

Serves 6

1 T. unflavored gelatin
2⅓ cups cold water
¾ cup boiling water
⅔ sugar, divided
1 cup milk
1½ tsp. almond extract
    food coloring
    fruit
    mint garnish

Soften gelatin in ⅓ cup cold water. Add boiling water and ⅓ cup sugar. Stir until dissolved. Add milk, extract and food coloring (to desired shade). Mix and pour into dish, chill until set. Cut into ½-inch cubes. Mix ⅓ cup sugar, 2 cups water and ½ tsp. extract. Divide gelatin squares and syrup among 8 bowls. Serve with fruit and garnish with mint.

Note: A few drops of yellow food coloring added to gelatin mixture is very attractive when served with blueberries. But use your imagination.

Almond Custard Filling

Yields 2½ cups

½ cup sugar
⅓ cup flour
½ tsp. salt
2 cups milk
2 eggs, beaten
2 tsp. almond extract

Mix sugar, flour and salt in saucepan. Stir in milk. Cook, stirring until it boils. Boil 1 minute. Remove from heat. Stir a little over half of mixture into eggs. Blend into hot mixture in saucepan. Bring just to boiling, Cool and blend in almond extract. Store in refrigerator.

Note: This rich custard may be put in cream puffs, shells, tarts, tortes or eaten on its own, topped with fruit. Delicious!

Microwave Pudding

Serves 4

- 2 cups half-and-half
- ¼ cup sugar
- 2 T. cornstarch
- 1 tsp. almond extract

Combine all but extract in microwave safe bowl. Stir. Ingredients will be lumpy. Microwave on high for 2 minutes. Whisk, microwave on high for 3 minutes. Stir in extract. Chill and serve.

Natillas

Serves 8

- 4 eggs, separated
- ¾ cup sugar
- ¼ cup flour
- 4 cups milk
- ½ tsp. almond extract
- ⅛ tsp. nutmeg

Beat egg yolks and stir in sugar and flour. Mix until smooth. Put milk and yolk mixture in saucepan; cook until mixture thickens to soft custard consistency. Remove from heat, add extract and cool. Beat egg whites until stiff, fold into custard. Spoon into individual dishes; chill. Sprinkle with nutmeg before serving.

Pinkies

Serves 4

- 1 3-oz. package strawberry-flavored gelatin
- ¾ cup boiling water
- 1 10-oz. package frozen sliced strawberries
- 1 cup plain yogurt

In blender combine gelatin and water. Cover and blend on high speed for 20 seconds until gelatin is dissolved. Add strawberries and yogurt and blend until smooth. Pour into parfait glasses and chill 1 hour or more. Garnish with whipped cream and fresh strawberries, if desired.

Quicky Tortoni   Serves 12

1 quart vanilla ice cream,
　　slightly softened
½ cup dry macaroon
　　crumbs
¼ cup chopped candied
　　cherries
¼ cup mini semisweet
　　chocolate chips
1 T. brandy
½ cup whipping cream,
　　whipped

Place paper liners in muffin tin. Combine ice cream, macaroon crumbs, cherries and chips in large bowl. Stir brandy into whipped cream, then fold into ice cream mixture. Divide mixture among muffin cups. Freeze until firm, at least 15 minutes.

Strawberry and Cheese Tart   Serves 8

1⅓ cups flour
1 cup plus 3 T. sugar
½ cup butter or margarine
1 egg yolk
2 3-oz. packages cream
　　cheese, softened
5 cups strawberry halves
3 T. cornstarch
1 cup water
　　red food coloring,
　　　optional

Preheat oven to 300°. Combine flour and 1 cup sugar with butter. Whirl in a food processor until coarse crumbs form. Blend in egg yolk. Press dough over bottom and up sides of 11-inch tart pan with removable bottom. Bake until golden, 30 minutes. Cool. Spread cheese over bottom of crust. Arrange 4 cups berries on cheese. Mash remaining 1 cup of berries. In a 2-quart pan, combine 1 T. sugar and cornstarch. Blend in mashed berries, water and a few drops of red food coloring. Stirring, bring to a boil and cook until glaze is thick and clear, 1 minute. Spoon glaze on berries. Chill 2 hours.

Mock Fried Ice Cream

Serves 4 to 6

¼ cup butter
½ cup graham cracker crumbs
4 cups corn flakes, crushed
1 tsp. cinnamon
2 dashes nutmeg
½ cup (packed) brown sugar
¼ cup ground almonds
1 pint ice cream
chocolate sauce

Melt butter. Add remaining ingredients and mix well. Press crumb mixture on ice cream and serve with Simply Splendid Chocolate Sauce (see Index).

Note: Dessert may be made before dinner and held in the freezer until 15 minutes before serving time.

Swiss Roll with Strawberries

Serves 10

½ cup sugar
3 eggs
½ cup flour
2 T. baking powder
1 cup whipped cream
1 lb. strawberries, mashed
powdered sugar
whole strawberries

Preheat oven to 350°. Beat sugar and eggs, gradually add flour and baking powder. Place wax paper on 11 x 15-inch pan. Butter wax paper and pour batter in pan. Bake 8 minutes or until golden. Sprinkle with powdered sugar, cover with wax paper and turn cake over to remove from pan. Remove top wax paper. Cool. If desired, sweeten whipped cream and strawberries. Combine cream and berries and spread on cake. Roll, jelly roll style. Sprinkle with powdered sugar and garnish with whole strawberries.

Luscious Lemon Sauce   **Yields 2 cups**

4 large lemons, use rind
    of one lemon
2 cups sugar
¾ cup butter
4 eggs, slightly beaten

Grate rind of one lemon. Squeeze lemons and strain juice. Put juice, sugar and butter in saucepan; cook over low heat until sugar and butter are melted. Remove from heat, add eggs slowly. Return to heat and cook until mixture coats spoon.

Note: Keeps in refrigerator 3 months.

Pineapple Pudding   **Serves 10 to 12**

1 cup butter, softened
2 cups sugar
3 eggs, slightly beaten
9 slices day-old bread,
    cubed
1 20-oz. can crushed
    pineapple, undrained

Preheat oven to 350°. Cream butter and sugar. Add eggs, bread and pineapple. Pour into 13 x 9 x 2 inch baking pan. Bake 1 hour until brown on top. Serve warm.

Note: Freezes well. For half recipe use ½ cup butter, 1 cup sugar, 2 eggs, 4 slices of bread and an 8-oz. can of pineapple.

Simply Splendid Chocolate Sauce
Yields 3 cups

1 12-oz. can evaporated
    milk
2 cups sugar
2 squares (1 oz. each)
    unsweetened baking
    chocolate
1 tsp. vanilla

Combine milk, sugar and chocolate in saucepan. Boil 5 minutes, stirring constantly. Remove from heat. Add vanilla. Beat with beater for 1 minute. Serve warm or store in refrigerator.

Chocolate Candy Logs

Yields 50 logs

1 cup melted butter
1 lb. powdered sugar
1 cup coconut
1 cup chopped nuts
1 tsp. vanilla
1 cup graham cracker
  crumbs
½ cup peanut butter
6 oz. (1 cup) chocolate
  chips
2 T. butter or margarine

Mix 1 cup melted butter, sugar, coconut, nuts, vanilla, crumbs and peanut butter. Roll into logs. Place on waxed paper and freeze. Melt chips and 2 T. butter. Dip frozen logs in chocolate and return to sheet. When frozen, cover and store in freezer or refrigerator.

Chocolate Nut Clusters

Yields 70

1¾ cups sugar
1 cup cream or canned
  evaporated milk
18 caramels, unwrapped
1 cup chocolate chips
3 cups salted, mixed nuts

In a saucepan melt sugar with cream and caramels. Cook 5 more minutes. Remove from heat. Add chocolate chips and stir until combined. Cool 10 minutes. Stir in nuts. Drop onto waxed paper; cool. Store tightly covered in a cool location. Do not refrigerate.

Dipped Chocolate Candy

Yields 4 dozen

½ cup butter or margarine
2 lb. powdered sugar
10 oz. Maraschino cherries
  drained and chopped
2 cups chopped nuts
1 14-oz. can sweetened
  condensed milk
1 cup coconut
1 cup chocolate chips

Melt butter and mix with sugar, cherries, nuts, milk and coconut. Form into balls and freeze on wax paper. Melt chocolate and coat candies. Dry on waxed paper.
Note: Butter and chocolate can be melted in microwave oven. Freezes well.

Chocolate Nut Candies   Yields 2 lb.

2 cups semi-sweet
     chocolate chips
1 14-oz. can sweetened
     condensed milk
2 cups rice cereal
1 cup peanuts

In microwave safe bowl combine chips and milk. Microwave on high for 3 minutes or until milk is hot and chips are melted. Stir vigorously. Add cereal and nuts. Drop by spoonfuls onto waxed paper. Chill 2 hours or until firm.

Creme de Menthe Squares   Yields 100 candies

1¼ cups butter or
      margarine
½ cup cocoa powder
3½ cups powdered sugar
1 egg, beaten
1 tsp. vanilla
2 cups graham cracker
      crumbs
⅓ cup green creme de
      menthe
1½ cups semisweet
      chocolate pieces

BOTTOM LAYER: In saucepan combine ½ cup butter and cocoa. Heat and stir until blended. Remove from heat; add ½ cup sugar, egg and vanilla. Stir in crumbs. Mix well. Press into bottom of ungreased 13 x 9-inch pan. MIDDLE LAYER: Melt ½ cup butter. In small mixer bowl combine butter and creme de menthe. At low speed of mixer beat in remaining 3 cups sugar until smooth. Spread over chocolate layer. Chill 1 hour. TOP LAYER: In small saucepan combine the remaining ¼ cup butter and chocolate pieces. Cook and stir until melted. Spread over mint layer. Chill 1 to 2 hours. Cut into small squares. Store in refrigerator.
Note: Freezes well.

Coconut Cherry Bonbons   Yields 2½ lb.

1 14-oz. can sweetened
   condensed milk
1 14-oz. can flaked
   coconut
1 6-oz. package cherry
   flavored gelatin
1 cup ground almonds
1 tsp. almond extract
   red food coloring

Combine milk, coconut, ⅓ cup gelatin, almonds and extract. Add red food coloring if you wish. Chill 1 hour until firm. With about ½ T., form into cherry shapes. Roll cherry in remaining gelatin to coat. Place on waxed paper and refrigerate.

Peanut Butter Cream Fudge   Yields 1 lb.

3 cups sugar
3 T. light corn syrup
1 cup milk
¼ tsp. salt
½ cup butter
1 cup plus 2 T. creamy or
   crunchy peanut
   butter
1 pint marshmallow
   creme
1½ tsp. vanilla
¾ cup milk chocolate
   chips

Grease cooking utensils. Mix sugar, syrup, milk and salt. Heat on medium high burner for 15 minutes or until mixture forms soft ball stage. Remove from heat and add butter, peanut butter, marshmallow cream and vanilla. Beat with wooden spoon until mixed. Pour into pan. Top with chocolate chips, press firmly into fudge mixture. Cool, then chill in refrigerator an hour until cold, about one hour.
Note: Freezes well. Recipe can be doubled.

Easy Walnut Toffee

Yields ½ lb.

½ cup butter
1 cup sugar
½ tsp. salt
¼ cup water
1½ cups chopped walnuts
1 cup semi-sweet
        chocolate chips

Butter 9-inch square pan. Melt butter in sauce pan. Gradually stir in sugar and salt; add water. Cook stirring occasionally to 290° or hard ball stage. Add 1 cup nuts, cook 3 minutes more, stirring constantly. Pour into pan. When cold, remove toffee from pan. Melt chocolate and coat one side of toffee. Sprinkle with nuts. Allow to set for a minute or so. Flip over on to waxed paper and repeat with chocolate and nuts. Break into bite-sized pieces.

Jelly Strings

Yields 100 pieces

3 3-oz. packages flavored
        gelatin, any flavor
½ cup water
        powdered sugar

In pan combine gelatin and water. Boil and stir until gelatin is dissolved. Wet an 8-inch square pan with water. Pour gelatin mixture into pan. Cover with waxed paper. Chill several hours until firm. Loosen edges with knife. Remove gelatin from pan. Using scissors, cut into thirds. Cut each third into narrow strips ¼ inch wide. Roll cut pieces in powdered sugar. Store, covered, in cool place. *Note: This easy treat also can be made in the microwave oven. Fun project for kids.*

Microwave Mint Fudge

Yields 1¾ lb.

3 6-oz. packages chocolate
   chips
1 14-oz. can sweetened
   condensed milk
2 tsp. peppermint extract
1 cup chopped walnuts

Line 8-inch square pan with waxed paper. In microwave safe bowl place chips and milk. Microwave on high until chips are melted, 4 minutes. Mix well and add remaining ingredients. Spread evenly in pan. Chill several hours until firm. Peel paper from fudge and cut into squares.
Note: Freezes well. Great!

Marzipan, European-Style

Yields ½ lb.

1⅓ cups slivered almonds
1⅓ cups powdered sugar
 ½ tsp. almond extract
 2 T. water
2¼ cups powdered sugar
 1 T. slightly beaten egg
   white

Grind almonds in blender. In mixer beat almonds, 1⅓ cups sugar, extract and water until mixture forms a ball. Beat in remaining powdered sugar. Stir in enough egg white to form a clay-like dough. Tint with food coloring, if desired. Store in a covered container at room temperature.

Pecan Pralines

Yields ½ lb.

1 cup (packed) brown
   sugar
1 cup sugar
½ cup whipping cream
1 T. vanilla
1 cup pecans
   buttered wax paper

Mix sugars and cream in pan and cook to 236° (soft ball stage). Remove from heat, add pecans and vanilla. Stir until mixture begins to lose its glossiness. Pour by spoonfuls onto buttered wax paper.

Microwave Divinity

Yields ½ lb.

2 egg whites, room
   temperature
2½ cups sugar
½ cup light corn syrup
½ cup water
⅛ tsp. salt
1 tsp. vanilla
1 cup chopped nuts

Butter 9 x 9-inch pan. Beat egg whites until stiff. In 3-quart microwave safe bowl, microwave sugar, salt, syrup and water to a boil. Stir once. Cook to 260° without stirring. Pour slowly over egg whites, beating constantly. Beat until it loses its gloss. Add vanilla and nuts. Pour in pan or drop by spoonfuls on wax paper.
Note: Divinity has never been so simple to prepare, and it is so good!

Speedy Peanut Brittle

Yields ½ lb.

1 cup sugar
½ cup dark corn syrup
1½ cups roasted peanuts
1 tsp. margarine
1 tsp. vanilla
1 tsp. baking soda

In 1½ quart microwave safe bowl stir sugar and corn syrup. Microwave on high for 4 minutes. Stir in nuts. Microwave 3 minutes. Stir in margarine and vanilla. Microwave 1 minute. Temperature should reach 300° or hard ball stage. Do not use candy thermometer in oven during cooking. If temperature is below 300°, cook 2 minutes longer checking temperature after each minute. Stir in soda until light and foamy. Pour onto greased cookie sheet. Break into pieces when cool.

Chocolate-Dipped Soft English Toffee

Yields 1½ lb.

2 cups sugar
1 cup butter
¼ cup water
1 cup whipping cream, scalded
2⅔ T. white corn syrup
1 cup chocolate chips, melted
½ cup chopped nuts

Cook sugar, butter and water to 250° (firm ball stage). Add cream and syrup. Cook to 235° (soft ball stage). Cool to 110°. Gently mix until creamy (do not beat fast or butter will separate). Place in refrigerator to harden. Form into balls. Refrigerate about 15 minutes. Melt chocolate. Dip balls in chocolate, then roll in nuts.

Wonderful Walnut Truffles

Yields 24

1 cup semisweet chocolate chips
1 egg yolk
½ tsp. orange zest
1 cup plus 3 T. finely chopped walnuts
2 T. butter
2½ tsp. Brandy

In microwave, melt chocolate. Add egg yolk, zest, 3 T. of walnuts, butter and Brandy. Beat together for 2 minutes, until combined. Refrigerate until firm, at least 1 hour. Put remaining walnuts in a small bowl. Shape the truffle mixture into 1-inch balls and roll in the nuts. Place in paper cups to serve.

Note: Preparation time is 10 minutes, plus chilling time. These quick, easy, delicious truffles are well worth 10 minutes! Freezes well.

Gelatin Blocks

Yields 100 pieces

4 envelopes unflavored
   gelatin
3 3-oz. packages flavored
   gelatin, any flavor
4 cups boiling water

In large bowl, combine gelatins. Add boiling water and stir until gelatin dissolves. Pour into 9 x 13-inch pan and chill until firm. Cut into 1-inch squares to serve. Store covered in refrigerator.
Note: Kids love these.

Speedy Toffee

Yields ½ lb.

1 cup chopped pecans
¾ cup (packed) brown
   sugar
½ cup butter
½ cup chocolate chips

Butter 8 inch pan and sprinkle with nuts. In 2 quart microwave safe bowl cook sugar and butter on high 4½ to 8½ minutes. Stir every 2 minutes. Cook to hard crack stage. Spread over nuts. Sprinkle chocolate chips over syrup mixture, let stand 20 seconds then spread. Cool and break into pieces.

Strawberry Candies

Yields 1 lb.

1 6-oz. package straw-
   berry gelatin
1 cup ground almonds
1 tsp. almond extract
2 cups flaked coconut
¾ cup sweetened
   condensed milk

Mix all ingredients; chill 1 hour. Shape into strawberries and coat with additional gelatin or sugar, if desired. Refrigerate or freeze.
Note: Decorate with green frosting for hull if desired.

Potpourri

SUNDOWN IN SAN JOSE

A nearly deserted village located between Santa Fe and Las Vegas, New Mexico, San Jose was once the site of the Pecos River crossing on the historic Santa Fe Trail. The picturesque old adobes and mission church are a wonderful subject in the winter snow.

Remoulade Sauce

Yields 3 cups

4 T. lemon juice
4 T. vinegar
4 T. prepared mustard
1 tsp. salt
½ tsp. black pepper
2 tsp. paprika
   dash cayenne
2 T. ketchup
1 cup salad oil
½ cup celery, chopped
½ cup green onions,
   minced

Combine lemon juice, vinegar and seasonings. Gradually add oil. Whisk until well blended. Add celery and onion.

Note: This sauce keeps in the refrigerator several days. It is delicious served on shrimp.

Versatile Cheese Sauce

Yields 3 cups

4 T. butter
4 T. flour
¼ tsp. pepper
½ tsp. dry mustard
½ tsp. Worcestershire
   sauce
⅛ tsp. nutmeg
2 cups milk
½ cup grated Cheddar
   cheese
1 5-oz. jar Old English
   cheese spread

In saucepan melt butter and blend in flour and seasonings. Cook over low heat, stirring until mixture is smooth and bubbly. Remove from heat and stir in milk. Bring to boil, stirring constantly. Boil 1 minute. Add cheese and cheese spread, mixing until smooth.

Note: Very good on vegetables, rice, macaroni and egg dishes. Variation: Add 2 T. Sherry and top fish fillets.

Cream Supreme

Yields 2 cups

1   8-oz. package cream
      cheese
2   T. lemon juice
1   tsp. lemon rind
½   cup whipping cream
½   cup powdered sugar

Mix cream cheese, lemon juice and rind. Whip cream to soft peaks and add sugar. Fold all ingredients together and serve with fruit. Store in refrigerator.

Pesto

Yields 2 cups

3   cloves garlic, minced
1   cup fresh basil
1   cup fresh parsley
½   cup olive oil
2   tsp. salt
1   tsp. pepper
½   cup pine or pinon nuts
½   cup fresh spinach
⅓   cup Parmesan cheese

Place all ingredients in food processor container. Process until smooth, adding more oil, if needed for consistency. *Note: Keeps refrigerated several weeks; freezes well. Can be used as a dip for vegetables or as a sauce for cooked pasta or vegetables. Makes a lovely lasagna when a layer of tomato sauce is replaced with a layer of pesto.*

Terrific Taco Sauce

Yields 1½ cups

1   8-oz. can tomato sauce
4   T. diced green chile
1   T. minced dried onions
½   tsp. ground cumin
½   tsp. ground oregano
1   tsp. salt
2   cloves garlic, minced
2   tsp. vinegar
1   T. lemon juice

Combine all ingredients.
Note: This sauce is very versatile and takes little time to prepare. It can be made ahead and kept refrigerated for up to a week. Taco sauce is great on tacos, burritos, eggs; can be used as a dip with tortilla chips. If you like a hot taco sauce, use jalapeno chilies. If you prefer a milder sauce, use mild green chile.

Mixed Nut Crunch

Yields 1½ quarts

4 quarts popped popcorn
2 cups dry roasted mixed
    nuts
1¼ cup sugar
⅔ cup butter or margarine
⅔ cup dark corn syrup
1 tsp. vanilla
½ tsp. baking soda

Preheat oven to 250°. Spread popcorn and nuts in large baking pan. Mix sugar, butter and corn syrup. Cook over medium heat stirring until mixture boils. Continue cooking 5 minutes without stirring. Remove from heat. Stir in vanilla and soda. Pour syrup over popcorn and nuts. Stir to coat. Bake uncovered for 1 hour. Stir occasionally. Cool. Break apart. Store in air tight container.
Note: The only way this keeps is if you hide it!

Six Minute Microwave Sweet Bridge Mix

Yields 2½ quarts

1 cup butter or margarine
½ cup white sugar
1 cup brown sugar
1 tsp. vanilla
½ tsp. baking soda
8 cups mixed cereals and
    pretzels
1 cup nuts

In 1-quart microwave safe bowl, melt butter. Add sugars and boil for 1 minute. Add vanilla and soda, and mix until foamy. Put cereals, pretzels and nuts in 9 x 13-inch microwave safe dish. Pour butter mixture over cereals and mix to coat. Microwave on high for 6 minutes, stirring every 2 minutes. Cool. Store in air-tight container.

SOUTHWEST SEASONS SOUTHWEST SEASONS SOUTHWEST SEASONS SOUTHWEST SEASONS SOUTHWEST

Poppy Cock

Yields 4 quarts

1 cup butter
1 cup corn syrup
1½ cups sugar
1½ cups nuts
1 tsp. vanilla
4 quarts popped popcorn

In a saucepan combine butter, corn syrup and sugar. Bring to boil and boil for 5 minutes. Remove from heat. Stir in vanilla and nuts. Pour over popcorn, mixing well to coat.

Southern New Mexico Pecans

Yields 1 lb.

½ cup butter
1 lb. pecans
½ cup whiskey
3 T. soy sauce
2 tsp. salt
8 drops hot pepper sauce

Melt butter in frying pan. Spread pecan halves in pan. Saute slowly until pecans are lightly browned. Stir in whiskey and simmer for 1 minute. Add soy sauce, salt and hot pepper sauce. Stir. Cool pecans on paper towels. Store in airtight container.

Sugared Pecans

Yields 3 cups

1 cup sugar
½ cup water
½ tsp. salt
2½ cups pecans
1½ tsp. vanilla

Mix sugar, water and salt with wooden spoon. Cook without stirring until candy thermometer reaches 224° (soft ball stage). Add pecans and vanilla and stir until nuts are coated and mix becomes creamy. Turn out on waxed paper. Cool; break apart.
Note: Delicious!

Cranberry Ice

Yields 1 quart

1 1-lb. can jellied
   cranberry sauce
1 cup lemon-lime soda
   Mint leaves

Beat cranberry sauce 5 minutes until smooth. Fold in soda. Freeze until almost firm. Transfer to food processor and mix until frothy. Turn into container, cover and freeze until ready to use. Garnish with mint leaves.

Note: Palate refresher. Very pretty around Christmas.

Lemon Refresher

Yields 1 quart

2 cups lemon juice
2 cups water
2 cups sugar

Combine all ingredients in saucepan and bring to boil, stirring constantly. Remove from heat, cool and freeze.

Note: Can be made weeks ahead and held in freezer. Stays soft enough to scoop while frozen. Nice served in small quantities before dinner.

New Mexico Green Chile Jam **Yields 1 pint**

½ cup water
¼ cup cider vinegar
2 cups sugar
1 cup diced green chile
1 1¾-oz. fruit pectin

Combine ingredients and boil 30 minutes. Cool and store in refrigerator or freezer.

Note: Chile Jam is especially good served on wheat crackers with cream cheese.

Bread and Butter Pickles

Yields 1 gal.

25 to 30 cucumbers
4 large onions
2 large green peppers
½ cup salt
5 cups vinegar
5 cups sugar
2 T. mustard seed
1 tsp. turmeric
½ tsp. cloves
2 tsp. celery seed

Wash and slice cucumbers. Chop onions and peppers. Layer cucumbers, onions, peppers and salt. Let stand 4 hours or overnight, then drain. Heat vinegar, sugar and spices to boiling. Add cucumbers, heat thoroughly but do NOT boil. Pour into sterilized jars and seal.

Green Tomato Pickles

Yields 1½ gal.

13 lb. green tomatoes
6 large onions
6 red bell peppers
1 cup salt
2 quarts vinegar
2 lb. brown sugar
¼ lb. mustard seed
1 oz. celery seed
1 tsp. allspice
1 tsp. mace
1 tsp. cloves
2 T. black pepper

Grind tomatoes with onions and peppers. Add salt. Let stand overnight. Drain. Add vinegar, sugar and spices to tomato mixture in large kettle and boil for 15 minutes. Can in sterilized Mason jars.

Spiced Pineapple

Yields 1 pint

1 20-oz. can pineapple, slices or chunks
¾ cup vinegar
1¼ cup sugar
6 to 8 whole cloves
1 4-inch piece stick cinnamon

Drain pineapple and reserve juice. To ¾ cup pineapple juice, add vinegar, sugar and spices. Heat. Add pineapple. Simmer 10 minutes. Cool. Refrigerate.
Note: Good with ham or pork.

Herb Butter

Yields ½ cup

2 T. chopped parsley
½ tsp. oregano
2 T. grated Parmesan
  cheese
⅛ tsp. garlic salt
½ cup butter, softened

Combine all ingredients. Store in refrigerator.
Note: Top vegetables or breads with this tasty butter.

Sweet Butter

Yields ¾ cup

½ cup butter, softened
¼ cup honey

Beat ingredients until fluffy. Store in refrigerator.

Low Sodium Spicy Seasoning

Yields ½ cup

2 T. dried savory,
  crumbled
1 T. dry mustard
2½ tsp. onion powder
1¾ tsp. curry powder
1¼ tsp. white pepper
1¼ tsp. ground cumin
½ tsp. garlic powder

Combine all ingredients in small bowl and blend well. Spoon into shaker. Store in a cool place.
Note: About 0.59 mg sodium per tsp.

Low Sodium Mild Seasoning

Yields ½ cup

2 T. dried dillweed or
  basil, crumbled
2 T. onion powder
1 tsp. dried oregano
  leaves, crumbled
1 tsp. celery seed
¼ tsp. grated dried lemon
  peel
  pinch pepper

Combine all ingredients in small bowl and blend well. Spoon into shaker. Store in cool place.
Note: About 0.65 mg sodium per tsp.

Coated Nuts

Yields 1½ quarts

4   cups shelled nuts
1   cup sugar
    dash of salt
½   cup butter
2   egg whites, beaten stiff

Preheat oven to 325°. Toast nuts until golden. Add sugar and salt to egg whites. Continue beating until stiff peaks form. Fold nuts into meringue. Melt butter in 11 x 15-inch pan. Spread nut mixture over butter. Bake 30 minutes stirring 3 times until nuts are coated and no butter remains. Separate nuts as much as possible to cool.
Note: Store in refrigerator or freeze.

Microwave Dog Biscuits
(For Pampered Pets)

Yield 18 cut-outs

1   cup whole wheat flour
½   cup flour
¾   cup dry milk powder
½   cup quick oats
¼   cup yellow cornmeal
1   tsp. sugar
⅓   cup shortening
1   egg
1   T. instant chicken or
      beef bouillon
½   cup hot water

Combine flours, milk, oats, cornmeal and sugar in bowl. Cut in shortening until mix is coarse crumbs. Stir in egg, bouillon and water. Stir to moisten. Form into ball and knead. Divide in half and roll ½ inch thick. Cut out with cookie cutters or make into nuggets. Put 6 shapes or 24 nuggets on 10-inch microwave safe plate. Microwave on medium power for 5 to 10 minutes, until firm and dry. Rotate plate every 2 minutes and turn shapes over after half the time. Cool on wire rack. They crisp as they cool.

Prominent People
and Restaurants

WINTER TWILIGHT AT THE KIVA

On the road to Chimayo, the tiny pueblo of Nambe with its scattered adobes, has as its center point one of the loveliest Kivas in New Mexico. Situated near Nambe Creek, the Kiva and the plaza where it stands are the site of the pueblo's ceremonies and dances.

Caesar Salad   Serves 8

Barbara Bush

2-3 cloves of garlic
 ½ cup olive oil
  4 cups bread cubes, ¼
      inch square
  4 quarts assorted lettuce
      greens
  1 cup grated Parmesan
      cheese
  1 tsp. salt
 ½ tsp. pepper
 12 tsp. olive oil
 ½ cup crumbled bleu
      cheese
  1 egg
  7 T. lemon juice
  2 T. Worcestershire sauce

Cut garlic into quarters and let sit in ½ cup olive oil overnight (out of refrigerator). Put bread cubes into shallow pan. Toast in 300° oven for 30 minutes until golden brown, turning with fork. After cooling, wrap in waxed paper until needed. Sprinkle lettuce greens with Parmesan cheese, bleu cheese, salt and pepper. Add olive oil (not oil treated with garlic). Mix together one egg, lemon juice, and Worcestershire sauce. Pour over salad and toss. Add croutons, flavored with garlic and oil mixed beforehand, to salad and toss. Do just before serving, as croutons get soggy.

Zucchini Soup   Serves 6 to 8

Barbara Bush

  1 lb. zucchini, cleaned but
      not peeled
1¾ cups chicken broth, or 3
      bouillon cubes
  2 T. shallots
  1 clove garlic, minced
  2 T. butter or margarine
  1 tsp. curry powder
 ½ tsp. salt
 ½ cup half-and-half

Chop zucchini, shallots and garlic. Put all three into a heavy frying pan with butter. Cook for 10 to 20 minutes. Stir to keep from burning; do not brown. Put all ingredients into blender and blend. Add half-and-half. Heat and serve hot with croutons, or chill and serve cold with chives.

Blackened Redfish
Serves 6

Barbara Bush

3	lb. redfish, filleted
	butter or margarine,
	melted
1	T. paprika
2½	tsp. salt
1	tsp. onion powder
1	tsp. red pepper
1	tsp. garlic powder
¾	tsp. white pepper
¾	tsp. black pepper
½	tsp. dry thyme
½	tsp. oregano

Dip fish in melted butter or margarine and then in mixture of seasonings. Cook in cast iron skillet, preheated until pan is very hot. Cook 2 minutes on one side, turn, and cook for another minute. *Note: This dish is very smokey to prepare; it cooks well outside on a grill or camp stove.*

Lemon Bars
Yields 3 dozen

Barbara Bush

1	cup margarine
2	cups powdered sugar
2	cups plus 4 T. flour
4	tsp. lemon juice
	rind of 2 lemons, grated
4	eggs, well beaten
2	cups sugar
1	tsp. baking powder
1	cup shredded coconut,
	optional

Preheat oven to 350°. Mix margarine, powdered sugar and 2 cups flour. Spread out in a jelly roll pan. Bake for 15 minutes or until pale tan. Mix lemon juice, rind, eggs, sugar, baking powder, 4 T. flour and coconut and pour over crust. Bake for 25 minutes.
Note: Mrs. Bush tells us that this is a recipe for "Lemon Lovers of America!" This is a favorite of the President Bush Family.

Mexican Cornbread
Serves 8 to 10

Marilyn Tucker Quayle

3 cups cornbread mix
3 eggs, beaten
2½ cups milk
1 large onion, grated
½ cup chopped jalapeno chilies
1½ cups grated longhorn cheese
6 slices bacon, cooked and crumbled
½ cup chopped pimento
½ cup bacon drippings
1 cup cream style corn
1 clove garlic, minced

Preheat oven to 375°. Mix all ingredients, pour into two large iron skillets and bake for 35 to 45 minutes.

Note: This special cornbread is enjoyed by the whole Quayle Family.

Governor's Mansion Chicken Enchilada Casserole
Serves 6 to 8

Governor Bruce King, New Mexico

1 4-oz. can chopped green chile
1 10-oz. can enchilada sauce
1 10¾-oz. can cream of chicken soup
1 5-oz. can evaporated milk
2 cups chicken broth
1½ dozen corn tortillas
2 cups grated longhorn cheese
2 T. chopped onion
1 stewing chicken, cooked, boned and chopped

Saute onions and chile in butter. Combine all liquids and add onion and chile. Break tortillas into pieces, place in casserole in layers with chicken and cheese, ending with cheese. Pour liquid over all and refrigerate overnight, or several hours. Bake at 350° for 1 hour.

Red Chile con Torta　　　Serves 6
Lt. Governor Casey E. Luna, New Mexico

18　red chile pods
3　cups water
2　T. flour
2　T. cooking oil
4　garlic cloves, crushed
　　salt
3　eggs
1　T. cracker crumbs

Wash and dry red chile pods; remove stem and seeds. Place pods on cookie sheet. Bake at 350° until pods are soft but not brown. Put pods in blender, add water, and puree until paste formed. Mix flour and oil, and rue (brown). Add chile puree, bring to boil, and simmer to consistency of gravy. Add crushed garlic and salt to taste. Simmer an additional one-half hour. Separate eggs. Beat egg yokes and add cracker crumbs. Beat egg whites until stiff, and fold egg yokes into egg whites. Drop mixture by tablespoonful into hot grease. Brown on each side. Put on paper towel to drain. After all patties are drained, put patties into red chile. Excellent served with beans and tortillas.

Banana Pineapple Cake

Serves 8 to 10

US Representative Steve and Marcia Schiff, New Mexico

3 cups sifted flour
1 tsp. baking soda
1 tsp. cinnamon
2 cups sugar
1 tsp. salt
1½ cups cooking oil
1 8-oz. can crushed pineapple, with juice
1½ tsp. vanilla
3 eggs
2 cups diced ripe bananas
1 cup chopped nuts

Preheat oven to 350°. Grease and flour 10-inch tube pan. Measure and sift dry ingredients. Add bananas to dry ingredients along with oil, vanilla, eggs, nuts and pineapple. The mixture is stirred to blend (but not beaten). Pour into pan and bake for 1 hour and 20 minutes. Cool in pan.

Scallop Casserole

Serves 4

US Representative Joe Skeen, New Mexico

24 oz. scallops
¼ cup chopped onion
2 T. butter
1 10¾-oz. can cream of mushroom soup
½ cup milk
½ to 1 tsp. curry powder
dash pepper
1 cup shredded cheddar cheese
1 lb. can French green beans
1 cup soft bread crumbs
2 T. butter, melted

Preheat oven to 425°. Simmer scallops in boiling salt water 3 minutes. Drain. Cook onion in butter until tender. Add soup, milk, curry, pepper and ½ cup of cheese. Stir until cheese melts. Slice scallops and combine with drained green beans in a 6 x 10 inch baking dish. Top with soup mixture. Sprinkle with remaining cheese, bread crumbs and melted butter. Bake for 20 minutes.
Note: Can be made ahead and refrigerated. Do not freeze.

Spaghetti Carbonara   Serves 4 to 6
President Richard E. Peck, University of New Mexico

4   T. butter, optional
2   whole eggs
2   egg yolks
1   cup grated Parmesan
    cheese
6   to 8 quarts water
1   tsp. salt
½   tsp. white pepper
1   lb. spaghetti
8   slices bacon, cut in ¼
    inch strips
1   tsp. dried red pepper,
    flakes
½   cup heavy cream
3   scallions, thinly sliced

1. Beat eggs and egg yolks with ½ cup Parmesan and white pepper. Set aside. 2. Heat water and cook spaghetti in boiling water for 10 minutes. 3. Fry bacon and scallions until bacon is crisp. Pour off half of bacon fat and add red pepper flakes, and then cream. Bring cream to a simmer and keep warm until spaghetti is done. When spaghetti is cooked, drain. Transfer to bowl and stir in butter, beaten eggs and hot bacon and cream mixture. The heat of the pasta will cook the eggs. Taste and season with salt and more Parmesan cheese. Serve.

Note: We lived in Rome for two years and this was my favorite. This can be made with skim milk, egg whites and turkey ham for the health conscious!

Bea's Salsa   Yields 1 quart
Albuquerque Councillor Bea Gutierrez

3   to 4 jalapenos
1   small onion
1   28-oz. can tomatoes
1½   tsp. garlic salt
1   tsp. cilantro

In blender chop onions, jalapenos and cilantro. Add garlic salt and tomatoes and blend briefly. Serve with corn tortilla chips.

Mrs. Hughes' Pie

Serves 6 to 8

Albuquerque Councillor & Mrs. Herb Hughes

1 unbaked 9 inch pie
  shell
½ cup margarine, melted
2 eggs, beaten
1 cup sugar
½ cup flour
1 tsp. vanilla
1 cup chocolate chips
1 cup chopped pecans

Preheat oven to 350°. Mix all ingredients and pour into shell. Bake for 45 minutes or until top is cracked. Serve warm with whipped cream on top.

Mexican Salad

Serves 6

New Mexico Representative Patricia V. Baca

1 lb. ground beef
½ head lettuce
1 cucumber
1 tomato
1 avocado
1 15-oz. can red kidney
  beans, drained
1 7-oz. package tortilla
  chips, crushed
1 8-oz. bottle Italian
  dressing
2 T. salsa

Brown beef and drain. Add beans to beef and simmer 5 minutes. Make salad while simmering. Add hamburger and beans to salad. Add tortilla chips, dressing and salsa and mix well.
Note: Salad can be doubled or tripled. Best to eat immediately while chips are crunchy.

Biscochitos

Yields 6 dozen

New Mexico Representative Barbara A. Perea Casey

1 lb. pure lard (2 cups),
   no substitute
1 cup sugar
2 eggs
2 tsp. anise
6 cups flour
3 tsp. baking powder
1 tsp. salt
1 cup wine
1 cup sugar, and 1 tsp.
   cinnamon - set aside

Cream sugar and lard. Add eggs and anise. Sift flour, salt, and baking powder and mix with lard mixture. Add enough wine to hold together (about 1 cup). Mix well. Roll dough out on floured board, ¼ inch thick. Cut into fancy shapes. Sprinkle with sugar and cinnamon mixture. Bake 15 minutes.

Note: Store in refrigerator or freeze. Great with hot chocolate or coffee.

Perfect Potato Casserole

Serves 12

New Mexico Representative Earlene Roberts

1 2-lb. package frozen
   hash browns, thawed
1 10½-oz. can cream
   chicken soup
2 cups grated cheddar
   cheese
2 cups sour cream
½ cup melted butter
½ cup chopped onion
   salt and pepper

Mix all ingredients. Place in greased 9 x 13-inch baking pan. Top with buttered corn flakes or bread crumbs. Bake at 350° for 45 minutes.

Note: Freezes well before or after baking. This dish is good for family meals as well as big parties. It's simple to make and delicious!

Curried Egg Dip

Yields 1½ cups

New Mexico Representative Jeannette Wallace

¼ tsp. Tabasco
½ tsp. curry powder
¼ tsp. dry mustard
½ tsp. salt
½ cup mayonnaise
1½ T. minced onions
½ cup minced celery
1 tsp. parsley
4 hard cooked eggs,
   minced

Mix and chill.

Note: Good with vegetable sticks.

Pistachio Marble Cake

Serves 10

New Mexico Representative Jeannette Wallace

1 18½-oz. package yellow
   cake mix
1 3-oz. package pistachio
   instant pudding
4 eggs
1 cup water
½ cup oil
1 tsp. almond extract
¼ cup chocolate syrup

Preheat oven to 350°. Grease and flour 10-inch tube pan. Mix all ingredients except chocolate syrup. Blend at medium speed for 2 minutes. Pour ⅓ of batter into separate bowl and stir in ¼ cup chocolate syrup. Spoon batter alternately into tube pan. Zig-zag spatula through batter to marble. Bake for 50 minutes or until center springs back when lightly touched.

Green Chile and Corn Chowder

Serves 12 to 18
Pat Keene, Artichoke Cafe, Albuquerque

4	T. butter or margarine
3	cups frozen corn kernels, thawed
1½	cups chopped green chile
3	onions, thinly sliced
4	potatoes, peeled and cut into ¼ inch dice
2	cups chicken stock
2	cups cream

Puree 2 cups corn in blender. Saute onions in butter until soft. Do not brown. Stir in corn puree, corn kernels, potatoes and stock. Bring to boil. Simmer, partially covered until potatoes are soft. Add chile, cream, salt and pepper to taste. Let simmer to reduce a little.

Santa Fe Black Bean Soup

Serves 6 to 8
La Fonda Hotel, Santa Fe

⅛	cup olive oil
⅛	lb. bacon, diced
⅛	lb. smoked ham, cut into 2 inch pieces
1	medium onion, chopped
2	cloves garlic, minced and pressed
2	stalks celery, chopped
1½	cups dried black beans
2½	tsp. dried ground red chile
4	cups water
	salt and pepper to taste
¼	cup Sherry wine
1	T. beef bouillon
1	tsp. cilantro
GARNISH:	
	sour cream
	guacamole
	chopped green onion

Heat oil in skillet. Add bacon, ham, onions, garlic and celery. Brown vegetables 40 minutes until soft. Add beans to pan with dried chile pepper, water and beef base. Bring to boil, reduce heat, cover and simmer 3 hours. Skim fat from top of soup. In food processor or blender puree mixture until smooth. Refrigerate until next day. When ready to serve add sherry and serve warm. Top with a dollop of sour cream, guacamole and green onion. *Note: Preparation time 1 to 1½ hours. Cooking time 3 to 3½ hours. Santa Fe frijoles negros, spicy and pureed, is a great party favorite.*

Capirotada (Sopa)
Santa Fe School of Cooking

Serves 6 to 8

12 to 14 slices day-old
    French bread
2 cups sugar
3⅓ cups water
1 tsp. cinnamon
5 T. butter
½ cup raisins
½ cup pinon or pecan nuts
1½ tsp. vanilla
1 cup shredded Jack or
    Longhorn cheese
    whipped cream for
    garnish
1 cup Madeira or sweet
    wine, optional

Preheat oven to 350°. Butter oven-proof baking dish. Tear bread into 1-inch pieces and toast in oven for 10 minutes. Place in mixing bowl; toss with bread and nuts. Place sugar in a saucepan over medium heat. Stir continuously with wire whisk until sugar melts and turns caramel color. Immediately add water, being very careful because the syrup will bubble and splatter. The caramel may partially solidify but will liquify as it reheats. Reduce heat and add raisins, butter and vanilla to caramel syrup while it is still hot. Continue to stir until butter has melted. Pour syrup mixture over bread mixture and soak well. Place mixture in the buttered baking dish. Top with cheese and bake for 30 minutes. Serve with whipped cream or ice cream. *Note: This recipe can be doubled or halved.*

Green Chili Clafoutis
Serves 8

Beauregard Detterman, N. Mex. Museum of Natural History

1 4-oz. can diced green
   chile, drained
1 tsp. baking powder
   pinch of salt
¾ cup milk
¼ cup sugar
4 eggs
2 cups flour
1 cup cheddar cheese

Preheat oven to 375°. Mix flour and baking powder in mixer. Make a well in the flour. Blend together eggs, sugar, milk and salt with flour at medium speed until completely smooth. Butter a 10 inch cake pan, preferably glass. Dust the pan lightly with flour. Pour chile and cheese in pan. Pour batter on top. Bake at 375° for 30 minutes. Reduce heat to 350° for 30 minutes. Let cool. Note: Serve warm for dessert. Can be made a day ahead.

Flan
Serves 6

La Fonda Hotel, Santa Fe

2 cups sugar
9 eggs
6 cups evaporated milk
2 T. vanilla
½ tsp. nutmeg
½ tsp. cinnamon
1 T. sugar
   whipped cream

Put two cups of sugar into a deep pan. Place over heat and stir constantly with a wooden spoon. Melt sugar until caramelized. Remove from heat and place into small bowls or large pan so it coats the inside. While sugar is being prepared, beat eggs with 1 T. sugar, milk, vanilla, nutmeg and cinnamon. Pour into containers. Place in a large flat pan with 1 inch water. Bake at 350° for 1 hour or until set. Cool. Invert on plate. Top with cream.

SOUTHWEST SEASONS SOUTHWEST SEASONS SOUTHWEST SEASONS SOUTHWEST SEASONS SOUTHWEST

Chicken en Croute   Serves 1

Stuart Robinson, la Cascada, Albuquerque

1   whole boneless chicken
      breast
¼   tsp. tarragon
1   clove garlic
4   inch puff pastry square
1   egg yolk
1   T. water
2   oz. heavy cream
1   oz. white wine
½   oz. mushrooms
      salt and pepper to taste

1. Slice garlic. 2. Place tarragon and garlic under skin of chicken. 3. Season chicken and form into a ball. 4. Pre-heat oven to 300°. 5. Place chicken in oven and cook for 10 minutes. 6. When chicken is cooked place in refrigerator to cool. 7. Make 1-inch cuts in puff pastry, leaving ¼ inch spaces between cuts. 8. When doing the second line of cuts, cut to the opposite side of the un-cut pastry to make a lattice. 9. Proceed with 7 and 8 until pastry square is covered. 10. When chicken is cold, wrap the pastry over the chicken and brush with egg-water mixture. 11. Bake at 300° until golden. For sauce: Fry mushrooms and season with salt and pepper. Add wine and cook until reduced by ½. Add cream and cook until reduced by ½. Season to taste.

Spicy Southwestern Chicken Crepe

Yields 12

Pat Keene, Artichoke Cafe, Albuquerque

CREPES FILLING:
- 1¼ cups sour cream
- ⅔ cup mayonnaise
- 3 T. fresh lime juice
- 1 to 2 bottles pickled jalapenos, drained, seeded and chopped
- 4½ cups cooked chicken, diced
- 4 plum tomatoes, seeded and chopped
- 2 cups chopped scallions
- ¼ cup chopped cilantro

CREPE BATTER:
- ¾ cup flour
- ⅓ cup cornmeal
- ½ tsp. salt
- 4 tsp. chili powder
- ¾ cups and 2 tsp. chicken broth
- 3 large eggs
- 1 T. butter, melted butter

Filling: In a bowl, stir together sour cream, mayonnaise, lime juice and jalapenos until smooth. Stir in chicken, tomatoes, scallions, cilantro and salt and pepper to taste. May be made 1 day ahead and refrigerated.

Chile Corn Crepe Batter: In blender or food processor, blend flour, cornmeal, salt, chili powder, broth, eggs and butter for 5 seconds. Scrape down edges and blend another 5 seconds. Transfer to bowl and let stand, covered for 1 hour. This may be refrigerated for 24 hours.

To Make Crepes: Heat nonstick 7 inch skillet over medium heat until hot. Brush pan with butter. Pour 2 oz. of batter into the pan. Tilt to cover bottom. Cook 1 minute. The crepe dries out and moves freely in pan. Turn with spatula. Cook other side lightly, and transfer crepe to plate. Make remaining crepes, brushing pan with butter as necessary. Stack and cover; may refrigerate 24 hours.

To Assemble Crepes: Preheat oven to 400°. Place crepe on plate. Put ½ cup filling in crepe and gently fold over. Transfer to buttered baking dish. Brush top with butter and bake 10 minutes. Transfer to plate. Garnish with sour cream, avocado slices and cilantro sprigs.

Galisteo Fiesta Salad with Black Bean Jicama Salsa   Serves 4

Vista Clara Spa Health Retreat

BLACK BEANS:
- 3 mild chilies, roasted, seeded and diced
- 1 onion
- ½ cup fresh cilantro
- 2 medium garlic cloves
- 2 tomatoes, seeded and diced
- 2 T. ground cumin
- 1 T. cayenne pepper

JICAMA SALSA:
- 1 carrot, grated
- 1 zucchini, grated
- 1 summer squash, grated
- 1 bunch scallions, diced
- 1 red onion, diced
- 3 tomatoes, seeded, diced
- 1 each red, yellow, green pepper, julienned then diced
- 1 cucumber, seeded, peeled, diced ¼ inch
- 1 medium jicama, peeled, cubed ¼-inch
- 2 bunches cilantro
- 3 cloves garlic, minced
- 3 T. Balsamic vinegar
- 3 T. canola oil
- 3 T. lime juice
  Dash chile sauce, medium hot
- 1 T. cayenne pepper
- 2 T. ground cumin
- 2 cups black beans (see recipe)

BLACK BEANS: Place beans in pot and cover with water. Bring to boil, then cover and allow to simmer. Add all other ingredients to beans. Gradually add water to beans during additional 2½ to 3 hours cooking time. Beans should remain covered with water until tender. Cool beans completely before adding to the jicama salsa.

JICAMA SALSA: Combine carrot, zucchini, summer squash, scallions, onion, tomatoes, peppers, cucumber and jicama in bowl with cilantro, oil, lime juice and vinegar. Add chile sauce and garlic to taste. If mixture needs more liquid, add juice of one tomato, additional lime juice, or more vinegar. Combine beans and salsa, and serve at room temperature over fresh garden greens; garnish with tomato wedges.

Note: This salad is excellent served as side dish to grilled entrees. Cilantro vinaigrette is a nice marinade or optional dressing. To keep calories down, stick with salad alone; it is a meal in itself.

Salmon Painted Desert   Serves 2
Vista Clara Spa Health Retreat

2 3-oz. salmon fillets
8.45 oz. soy milk
3 cloves garlic
¼ cup goat cheese
2 tsp. color pastels (see recipe)
1 cup yellow bell peppers, chopped
½ cup potatoes, peeled and diced
1 pinch saffron
1 cup chicken stock
½ cup water
1 tsp. oil, canola or vegetable
2 large cloves garlic, finely chopped
½ cup red chile pepper
¾ cup water

For sauce: Combine soy milk, garlic and goat cheese; simmer until cheese has melted. Slowly cook until thickened. Strain out garlic through fine sieve. Pour back into sauce pot, cover and keep warm.

For Salmon: Bring water to boil in steamer or large pot with steamer rack. Steam salmon for 5 to 7 minutes. Salmon should be slightly pink in center. Just before salmon is done, ladle sauce into middle of each warmed serving plate, tilting plate to coat it evenly. Using red Desert Pastel at one side of each plate, draw four or five lines, each 1 inch apart. Repeat with yellow Desert Pastel, alternating with red lines. With tip of knife, draw perpendicular lines about ½ inch apart through red and yellow pastel lines. Place salmon on half of plate nearest diner.

For yellow Desert Pastel: Simmer peppers, potatoes and saffron with the chicken stock and water for about 20 to 25 minutes in small covered pot. Place mixture in blender and puree to fine smooth texture. Pour into squeeze bottle and keep warm until ready to serve.

For red Desert Pastel: Heat oil in small skillet over moderate heat. Add garlic and saute for about 2 to 3 minutes. Do not brown. Place half of red chile pepper in the skillet, stirring constantly. Add remaining chile pepper while stirring. Immediately add water and stir until well blended. Remove skillet from heat; pour mixture into blender, and puree. Pour through a fine sieve. Refrigerate until needed.

Real New Mexico Salsa   Yields 2 cups
Bill Real, Gas Company of New Mexico

½ red onion, minced
½ tsp. garlic powder
¼ cup fresh chopped
   cilantro
1 T. cider vinegar
3-5 seeded fresh jalapenos
5 medium tomatoes,
   skinned and seeded
1 tsp. salt or to taste
½ cup tomato puree

Place all ingredients except puree in food processor. Chop. Stir in puree. Correct salt to taste. Chill at least ½ hour before serving with tortilla chips, etc.
Note: Heat level increases over time. Keeps well refrigerated or frozen.

Mexican Pineapple Cake   Serves 12 to 16
Bill Real, Gas Company of New Mexico

2 cups sifted flour
2 cups sugar
2 eggs
2 tsp. baking soda
1 20-oz. can crushed
   pineapple, including
   juice
1 cup chopped nuts
1 8-oz. package cream
   cheese
½ cup margarine
2 cups powdered sugar
1 tsp. vanilla

Preheat oven to 350°. Grease and flour 9 x 13-inch pan. Mix flour, sugar, eggs, soda, pineapple and nuts until well blended. Pour into pan and bake for 30 minutes or until toothpick inserted in cake comes out clean. For icing: set out cream cheese and margarine to soften. Mix together until smooth. Add remaining ingredients. Blend until smooth. Spread on cooled cake.

Contributors

Jean Adams
Terry Allahdadi
Ruth E. Andrews
Shanaz Arman
Madeline Arrington
Patricia V. Baca
Marilyn Batts
Anita Bettinger
Kathleen Bickel
Nancy Blankfield
Nelly Borchardt
Mimi Brannon
Katherine Browne
Valdia Buchwald
Louise Burk
Barbara Bush
Barbara A. Perea Casey
Carol Chiordi-Jones
John Chiordi
Carole Christensen
Martha Clark
Helen Cone
Betty Corwin
Gloria Crespin
Betty Cummings
Adele Davis
Beauregard Detterman
Ruby Lee Dolzadelli
Catherine Domenici
Eileen Doran
Theresa Doran
Ann Duggan
Mary Estepp
Janet Ferguson
Helene Cobas Fike
Dorothy Fitz-Gerald

Linda Franchini
Sherry Frese
Shari Friedman
Mary C. Garrison
Margaret Generosa
Helen Godfrey
Elizabeth Godfrey
Kathryn B. Godfrey
Lillian Godfrey
Mark Godfrey
Patricia Godfrey, R.D.
W. Berry Godfrey
Ellen Gottschalk
Bea Gutierrez
Nathana Haines
Cecilia Hansen
Rose Murphy Hansen
Janice Harker
Mary Harris
Denise Henderson
Barbara Henricksen
Imelda Hermosillo
Becca Hodges
Lindsey M. Hovden
Sandra Hovden
Grace Hsu
Mr. & Mrs. Herb Hughes
Betty Iames
Nancy Ingram
Angeline Jasper
Judy Johnson
Christie Kawal
Pat Keene
Kate Keith
Gretchen Keleher
Florence Kennedy

Alicia Fletcher
Dorothy Helen Ford
Jeri Laxson
Elise Lee
Virginia Long
Casey E. Luna
Janet Lyle
Carole Mahuron
Sandra Marchiando
Jan Margard
Christine Matalucci
Sue McCann
Betsey McCrory
Shirley McKnight
Leonor A. Mead
Muffin Menicucci
Susie Menicucci
Florence Metz
Louise Micsko
Cindy Miller
Lorna Miller
Cree Ann Morris
Janet Nadolny
Marie Nash
Pinkie Neff
Richard E. Peck
Lori Peterkin
Betsy Pobanz
Florence Pobanz
Katie Pooler
Mayme Proscia
Kathleen Raskob
Bill Real
Karen Remund
Stuart Robinson
Mary Ellen Rock
Darla Rossi

Bruce King
La Fonda Hotel
Mrs. J. W. Rogers
Maurita Rust
Mary Ruvolo
Sarah Ruvolo
Betty Sabo
Janet Sale
Santa Fe School of Cooking
Gwyn Schaefer
Steve and Marcia Schiff
Julia Y. Seligman
Vicki Serola
Shari Shaffer
Sister Paola
Joe Skeen
Marie Ethel Smith
Marjorie Stellingwerf
Shirley Straub
David Straw
Pixie Strovinskas
Inga Taylor
Kathy Thode
Elizabeth Thompson
Regina Thornton
Louise Turner
Sandra Tybor
Vista Clara Spa
Jacqueline Vodian
Becky Vokes
Pat Waldrip
Jeannett Wallace
Vesta Wheeler
Particia Whited
Carol Yonov
Rusty Yount
Catherine Ziler

Index

Index

SOUTHWEST SEASONS SOUTHWEST SEASONS SOUTHWEST SEASONS SOUTHWEST SEASONS SOUTHWEST

Southwest Seasons Cookbook

% Casa Angelica
5629 Isleta Blvd. S. W.
Albuquerque, New Mexico 87105

Please send me ___ Cookbooks $ 14.95 each _____
Postage and handling in U. S.   3.00 each _____
Gift wrapping (optional)   1.00 each _____
Total enclosed   _____

Name _____
Street _____
City _____ State _____ Zip _____

Please make checks payable to *Casa Angelica Auxiliary, Inc.*

Southwest Seasons Cookbook

% Casa Angelica
5629 Isleta Blvd. S. W.
Albuquerque, New Mexico 87105

Please send me ___ Cookbooks $ 14.95 each _____
Postage and handling in U. S.   3.00 each _____
Gift wrapping (optional)   1.00 each _____
Total enclosed   _____

Name _____
Street _____
City _____ State _____ Zip _____

Please make checks payable to *Casa Angelica Auxiliary, Inc.*